AN ADOPTION MEMOIR

Blessings!

Sharla.

THAT THESE TWO WILL LIVE

SHARLA KOSTELYK

THAT THESE TWO WILL LIVE

Printed in Canada

Word Alive Press
131 Cordite Road, Winnipeg, MB R3W 1S1
www.wordalivepress.ca

WORD ALIVE PRESS
Just Write!

Cover design by: Matt Aubin of Pure Vision Inc.

purevision

MIX
Paper from responsible sources
FSC   FSC® C016245
www.fsc.org

Library and Archives Canada Cataloguing in Publication
Kostelyk, Sharla, 1975-
That these two will live : an adoption memoir / Sharla Kostelyk.
ISBN 978-1-77069-412-5
1. Kostelyk, Sharla, 1975-. 2. Kostelyk, Mark. 3. Adoptive parents–Canada–Biography. 4. Adopted children–Ethiopia–Biography. 5. Intercountry adoption–Canada. 6. Intercountry adoption–Ethiopia. I. Title.
HV875.5.K67 2011 362.734092 C2011-907561-X

one

PEOPLE ALWAYS SAY THAT THE DAY THEIR LIFE CHANGED STARTED OFF LIKE any other, but Monday, July 13, 2009, did not start out just like any other weekday for us.

We were in a hotel room in Banff, Alberta, having spent the weekend there with my brother, his family, and my parents to celebrate my parents' fortieth anniversary. My parents had already left on what was to be a ten-day vacation. We had packed up and the door to our suite was being held open, as was the door across the hall, where my brother and his wife were making trips down to their vehicle with their bags and baby paraphernalia.

Most of our kids were already down in the parkade, where Mark had just carried the rest of our luggage. I was doing a last sweep of the rooms to ensure that we had everything when my cell phone rang. Given that we were hurrying to get on the road, I wouldn't have answered it except that I saw it was a number from British Columbia. Thinking it might be one of Mark's sisters, I picked it up.

As with all moments that change one's life, I remember clear details from that minute. I was in the kitchen of the suite, on my way to the door and within a few words of the call, Mark had walked back into the room. When he saw that I was on the

1

phone, he shot me a look as if to say, "We've got to get going." But then he must have seen the look on my face, because his expression quickly shifted to concern as I sunk down into one of the chairs at the small round table.

The voice on the other end of the phone belonged to my friend Justine, a friend who phoned only once or twice a year. Justine and I had met through the online world of blogging and, having much in common, had become friends in real life, too. During the previous year, we had met in person for the first time, when she and five of her kids had come to stay with us for a few days. Just a month earlier, they had come again. This time, she had brought seven of her kids along, including two girls from Ethiopia who ten months earlier had been added to her previously all-boy family.

However strange it may sound to some, we were not phone friends. With large families and busy lives, we communicated only through emails and our yearly visits, so her call, especially on my cell phone, meant that it was something important.

I don't remember her exact words, but they were something along the lines of, "Where are you? Have you been on your computer? Have you heard?"

I explained that I was in Banff and had had no access to a computer since early Friday. From the tone of her voice, I immediately felt fear.

"You have to go to Ethiopia, now," she said. "Your kids are in trouble."

I think that may have been the point when I sat down. I wasn't processing what she was saying very well. She was talking about rumors of our adoption agency, Imagine Adoptions, going bankrupt, and about parents who were already in Ethiopia to pick up their kids and were urging other parents to come immediately. She spoke about what was being said on the message boards, and then I heard the words that changed everything: "running out of food."

My body felt like I was no longer in it. It was like I could

see myself sitting on the chair, holding the phone, but it wasn't really me. I said very little to Justine and she kept urging me to go to Ethiopia or to have Mark go.

It was surreal. Moments earlier, I had been about to hop into the van to head home, our expected travel to Ethiopia not even in the forefront of our minds as it was at least three months away. Now here I was, hearing a friend urge me to go now, for reasons that seemed implausible.

Our adoption agency had hundreds of clients and a good reputation. They were a Christian agency with the tagline "Our unique total love approach," and we had chosen them largely because of the care that was given to the children waiting to come to Canada in their Transition Home in Ethiopia. At the time we chose them, there were two agencies in Canada facilitating adoptions in Ethiopia and we felt confident that we had chosen the one that was right for us.

I'd had contact with my caseworker at Imagine just the week before. Less than three weeks earlier, we had also received new pictures of our two Ethiopian children, in which they were smiling, giving no indication that anything had changed at the Transition Home where they were staying. I knew that just days prior, the agency had cashed checks from other adoptive parents. It was unfathomable that they were bankrupt or that our children were in danger.

Mark was trying to get my attention to find out what the heck was going on. I must have told him at some point, though I don't remember what I said. By then, my brother Matt was standing in our open doorway and Mark took him out in the hall to explain the little that we knew.

The night before, we had gone out for our parents' anniversary supper. At dinner, we had all decided that we would wait to take the family portrait that my brother, a photographer and graphic design artist, was gifting to my parents. We all agreed that it would be better to wait until the newest members of the family had arrived, either in late fall or winter. We had

3

joked about how amazing it was that with only two kids, my parents were going to have at least nine grandchildren.

Now, just thirteen hours later, two of those grandkids were at the center of this news. Matt came in and gave me a hug, said goodbye, and told Mark to call them when we knew more.

During this first call with Justine, I began a notebook that was to become my organizer and lifeline over the coming weeks. She gave me the phone number of a friend of hers who had adopted through Imagine before, was adopting through them again, and who might have more information. Justine also gave me the phone number for the driver they had used while in Ethiopia and a few other contacts from there.

I was already dialing the number for Justine's friend as we walked out of the hotel room and towards the parkade. She didn't have many more details, but she confirmed that the rumors did, in fact, seem true and that no one at Imagine's office in Cambridge, Ontario was answering the phone. At that point, there was a rumor circulating that Imagine was going to issue a public statement on Wednesday.

I gave Justine's friend my contact numbers and asked her to please call me as soon as she heard anything else.

Before we got off the phone, she told me that adoptive parents currently in Ethiopia were reporting that there were only three or four days of food left for the kids at the Transition Home and that there was no money for gas to get the kids to any appointments. None of the staff had been paid for at least six weeks. The staff and caregivers still there were taking care of our children out of kindness.

She urged me to get to Ethiopia as quickly as I could.

I believe it was somewhere in the stairwell or in the parkade when the tears came. Once I was sitting in the van, I was crying so hard that I couldn't answer the questions from my other kids. Mark explained to them that there was a problem in Ethiopia and that I was worried about their brother and sister, but that everything would be okay. I just sat there and sobbed.

4

Mark stopped at the hotel's office and went in to check us out. I stayed in the van and sobbed.

He came back and we drove through Banff. I sobbed some more. I felt like someone had punched me in the stomach, as I couldn't seem to get enough air. It was the most helpless I have ever felt in my life, knowing that two of my children were literally half a world away and in danger, but I couldn't help them. Even if I'd been able to get on a plane right away, it would have taken me three days to reach them.

It still amazes me how I truly became their mother in that first moment of Justine's phone call. Legally, I had become their mother just weeks earlier, on June 22, when a court in Ethiopia ruled that they were now officially our children. On that day, I was happy, relieved, and excited about the prospect of being their mother as I stared at their pictures for clues about who they were and how they would someday react to meeting me, but the full-on protective mother bear type of love didn't come until July 13! It came on with such force that it almost knocked me off my feet.

Mark is slightly more logical than I am, and perhaps a tad more even-keeled. I tend to swing more on the emotional side. He had largely been silent thus far, asking the occasional question, pointing out that we shouldn't panic until we knew for sure that these rumors were even true.

He reached over and held my hand while I cried and offered a few, "It's going to be okay" type of reassurances. For the most part, he was quiet, thinking.

On the highway past Canmore, he turned to me and said matter-of-factly, "I'll go."

We had already discussed all the reasons that he couldn't go. He was self-employed with no one to cover for him while he was away, we had five other kids, we had bills to pay and his income was needed, there would be expenses in Ethiopia, and it would probably be three or four months before he was able to come home.

But they were our children, just as much as the ones we could see in the backseat of the van, and we would do anything for any one of them. No matter the practical lunacy of it, we would do whatever it took to save our children.

His words were a turning point for me. I was still teary and emotional, but I knew that action was needed.

My first calls were to ask people to spread the word that these children needed immediate prayer. I said the words to our friends and family through tears but knew that the best hope our kids had was God's care. We couldn't be with them, but He could.

We stopped at a drive-thru in Cochrane to feed the hungry kids in the backseat. For the first time, I discovered that I couldn't entertain the idea of eating while wondering if my Ethiopian kids were starving.

Calling Mark's sister Deanne was especially hard. Deanne had become one of my closest friends over the years and the plan from the beginning had been for her to come to Ethiopia with Mark and I when we went to pick up the kids. However, we always knew that she wouldn't be able to come if the trip's timing fell in the summer months, because that was her busy season at work. With our original trip looking like it would happen in the late fall, the timing could not have been better for her to come along, and the three of us had spent many hours excitedly talking about plans.

Even as a young girl, Deanne had dreamed of going to Africa to help in an orphanage, so this trip was to be the fulfillment of her lifelong dream. She had been looking forward to this, and we had been looking forward to experiencing it with her, as well as having her company and help for the travel portion.

I knew that there wasn't any chance of her being able to come now that Mark was going right away, and it seemed unlikely that I would go at all.

When Deanne and I spoke, she only expressed concern for our kids and for our fears, but I knew that she had to be

disappointed for herself, too. In addition to eagerly anticipating her time in the orphanage, she had been excited to meet our new kids. She had followed every step along this adoption road, cheering every milestone along the way, printing out pictures of the kids for her fridge, and knowing that she would have the chance to form a special relationship with them by being there those first days. She had foreseen being able to be a special auntie in their lives, even though she lived in another province. Learning that she wasn't going to be able to go to Africa or be there to help us and meet the kids was devastating news.

I decided not to call my parents. My mom and I were extremely close and I knew that once she found out what was happening, she wouldn't be able to enjoy her vacation. She would want to be with us and help, so I asked my brother and his wife not to mention anything to her.

She did call me later that day, however, to see if we were on our way home and check how things were going. I fought back tears while I lied about being fine and told the truth about being on our way home. I wished her a great vacation, told her I loved her, hung up, and broke down again, wishing so much that I could have had my mom there to tell me that things were going to be okay.

CHAPTER

two

MARK AND I HAD FALLEN INTO THE ADOPTION WORLD NINE YEARS EARLIER. We both wanted a big family, Mark because he came from one, and me because I hadn't. During my pregnancy with our second son, Jonah, I experienced complications, resulting in many months in the hospital that necessitated being away from our older son, Mackenzie. My doctor felt that another pregnancy would be risky to my life and the baby's. Knowing that we wouldn't have any more biological children didn't dampen our hopes for a large family. I briefly grieved about not being able to carry another child, then moved naturally to thoughts of adoption.

Adoption didn't seem like a second option scenario to me, though. When I was in the fourth grade, I had a friend whose parents were foster parents and had adopted several special needs children. I only spent time with this girl and her family for one year, but it was enough to convince me that adoption, and maybe fostering, were in my future.

I always planned to adopt, and was excited about the expansion of our family. When Jonah was a baby, Mark went back to school, so we waited until he graduated and got a job before we applied for adoption. However, during the two years he spent studying, I did some studying of my own… researching

adoption. I researched all of our options, but though international adoption, and adoption from Africa in particular, did pull at me, it was not even a remote possibility.

With Mark having just graduated, leaving us with the burden of student loans, and having two children already, our finances could not sustain any adoption that wasn't free. We applied to adopt through our local government, and once our initial application was approved, the next step was to take a course that took four full Saturdays, where the geniuses at Alberta Child and Family Services were smart enough to group together all applicants for adoption, foster-to-adopt, and fostering. Over those four days, we heard all kinds of stories of children whose lives had been changed because of their placement in a loving and qualified foster home. We also heard of how large the need was for such homes. Children, even babies, were in hotels with workers who were rotating eight-hour shifts because of the shortage of foster homes.

On the way home from our third of four sessions, Mark turned to me in the vehicle and said, "You know, we're still young. Maybe we could help out more kids by fostering. Along the way, maybe we'd get to adopt some of them."

Mark had been very clear from the first time I brought up my childhood wish to someday foster that he would never be willing, and here he was suggesting it!

Over the next few weeks, we became aware of a private foster agency, Crossroads Family Services, whose values were similar to ours and who apparently had wonderful, caring staff and who put the interests of children first. We gave them a call. In just a few months, we completed our home study process and all of our criminal, reference, and background checks. We were soon staring into the beautiful green eyes of our first little foster daughter. Our eight years of fostering were full of adventure, interesting experiences, heartbreaks, and joys. Foster parenting had its blessings and challenges, but it brought us three of the children we now call our own.

On a cold December night, Gracelyn came to us at three days old, weighing less than five pounds and wearing only a diaper and a doll hat, hidden under a blanket in a carseat. She was carried into our home by the tallest police officer I have ever seen. She stole our hearts in a glance! We have learned more about compassion, optimism, and courage from her than from any other human being we have ever encountered.

Josiah came eight months later, at just six months old, already needing intervention for his attachment and development. He has grown into a brilliant boy who taught himself to read, enjoying how-to books the most, and is our family's Mr. Fix-it.

Gracelyn and Josiah became "the twins." Being just two months apart, their bond is incredible.

Three years later, with many foster children in between, we received the call about Gracelyn's birth sister. We were thrilled at the chance for them to be together and never even considered saying no. We named her Eliana. She came to us at twenty-four hours old, with her gorgeous blue eyes and dramatic actress qualities capturing the hearts of us all, especially Mackenzie and Jonah, her two oldest brothers.

At five children, three boys and two girls, our family was large by most standards, but I had always dreamed of having six. I had always felt drawn to adopt from Africa and was now able to convince Mark that one final adoption was a good idea.

Our adoptions through our province's foster care system had taken a long time to finalize. Josiah's was the most complicated and stressful, taking over five and a half years to complete from the time he was first living with us. From Josiah's point of view, we had always been his family and he was completely unaware that there was ever a risk to his security in being here. However, as adults, we lived through the uncertainties and even faced the possibility of having to say goodbye forever to a boy we thought of as our son.

The emotional rollercoaster took its toll. By the end, I didn't feel that I could endure starting a new situation of

foster-to-adopt—or, as some call it, legal risk adoption. With legal risk, it's actually your heart you risk…and it can be devastating. I believe in adopting from foster care or within foster-to-adopt, as it is the best possible outcome for the child involved.

There were still many children in our province and elsewhere who needed homes, but I didn't feel equipped to handle it again so soon after living through the unknowns with Josiah. Selfishly, I was looking for an adoption that would be easier and quicker. I thought international adoption was the way to achieve that.

I can laugh at my innocence now!

I spent months researching adoption programs and agencies and countries, but Ethiopia had me right from the start. When I saw the country name on an agency's website, I knew this was where our child was.

I attribute this largely to being a child raised in the 80s. I was growing up in the years of "We Are the World" and the 1984–1985 famine in Ethiopia. I was one of the many children raised in that era who, upon not finishing their dinner, would hear, "Don't you know there are starving children in Ethiopia?" How naïve I was! When I suggested we send the leftover food to them, my mom had to explain that by the time it got packed on a plane and taken to the people in the remote villages who needed it, it would have spoiled, so I just needed to eat it and appreciate it.

One day at the age of nine or ten, I saw a World Vision program on TV. I took in the images of starving children whose eyes seemed to show that they had lost all hope. I remember every child on the program that day. Their hopelessness haunts me still. I was home alone, and by the time my mom returned I had called the number at the bottom of the screen and pledged to sponsor a child. I don't think my mom was thrilled that I had committed to this without checking with her first, but she softened when I offered to pay for it with my allowance, though I don't recall her holding me to that.

11

I was thrilled when the sponsor child information came for a little boy living in Ghana. As a child growing up in an almost all-white community, I was drawn many other times to learning about Africa, and about the children in Ethiopia who were starving or sick. When I look back, I see that Africa called to me long before I heard it.

When I was first looking into adopting from Ethiopia, there was only one agency in Canada that facilitated adoptions there. It was a well-established agency with a solid reputation and years of experience working with Ethiopia. Mark and I discussed it and decided to go ahead.

We sent off the retainer fee and our initial application and applied to our province for approval. The agency sent us a fat binder full of great information, which I devoured immediately, but which Mark did not seem to want to crack open. At the time, it appeared to me that Mark was only lukewarm on the idea of this next addition to our family. I didn't want to proceed without him fully on board, so I let it just sit for about a year.

During that year, I didn't stay on the bench. I was actively involved in an online message board of others in Canada who had adopted from Ethiopia or who were in the process of adoption. I researched as much as I could about the country and the process, trying to learn, especially from others' experiences.

There were changes going on with our family that year, changes which made adding another family member seem more attractive than it had before, such as us moving to an acreage where there was plenty of room for the kids to roam around outside. Once we had the basement finished, there were seven bedrooms plus an office that could be converted to an extra bedroom if it was ever needed.

Our new house felt like a palace compared to the home we'd been in before. Eliana's crib had been set up in our walk-in closet due to lack of bedrooms! Mark was more established in his career now as well and we were no longer taking new foster children, so I wasn't surprised when Mark brought up the

"I will not leave you as orphans;
I will come to you."

To Mandi, without whom there would be no book as she lovingly looked after my children while I hibernated in the office to write it. She even brought me in tea and made sure that I was eating! I am so thankful that God brought you into my life and for the friendship we share, the real conversations we have had, and for the blessing that you are to our whole family. I really could not have done this without you.

To Deanne, who wished for our kids almost as much as we did and who made the trek to Ethiopia with us. You have always given me unconditional acceptance and I so value our friendship.

To Nell and John Kostelyk, my mom and dad (in-law) who are an incredible example to me of committed marriage (they just celebrated 55 years together), trusting the Lord, and loving without judgment.

To the online adoption community, from whom I have learned so much and within which I have made some lasting friendships. To the adoption professionals who helped with this adoption and with our other adoptions.

And of course, thank you to all those who helped with our adoptions, whether it be organizing fundraisers, donating items or their time at the garage sale, helping get our house ready for the kids, dropping off meals, or just providing a listening ear and supportive word...Denise, Glenda, Diane, Cyndie, Lorraine, Lyle and Grayce, David, Michelle, Shannon, and so many others.

Mackenzie, Jonah, Gracelyn, Josiah, Elijah, Eliana, and Sedaya, you have all been so patient while I wrote this book and I am happy to be able to keep my promise to you of taking you out to Ragazzi's and buying you all Slurpees from Macs to celebrate! You are the best kids in the world and I am so thankful for each one of you! You are my most treasured gifts.

acknowledgements

First and foremost, I need to thank God, who has blessed me with my seven precious children and is the author of my story, the giver of my life.

To Mark, who said "yes" to this big family and all the love and chaos that comes with it! You are the most amazing father and I wouldn't trade our life together for a "normal" life any day!

To Abebech, who gave life to two of our children and loved them well. I will forever be grateful.

To my mom, Mary-Lynne Aubin, my lifelong best friend Holly Kowalchuk, and Mandi Lister, who all believed from the start that I could somehow manage to write this in amongst my busy schedule and for all that they did to make sure that it happened. This would not have been possible without that support, encouragement, and practical help.

To my Auntie Judy Pichach and Ruth Branson for their time and encouragement. I so appreciate the two of them editing my first drafts and providing honest feedback.

To my brother Matt Aubin, who gave generously of his time and resources to help with many of the pictures featured in the book and to his company, Pure Vision Inc. who did a fabulous job of designing the book's cover.

subject again of one last adoption. Our family was stable and we felt capable of handling one more child.

During our years as foster parents, it wasn't uncommon for us to have a total of six kids at once. On one occasion, we even had six children under the age of eight, so I knew without a doubt that we could parent six. When our last little foster boy left, after having been with us for more than a year and a half, we had only five kids left—and it felt like someone was missing. Adding another seemed natural. Mark was now fully on board and we were ready to really pursue this.

In that year of hiatus, a change had come into the adoption world in Canada. While I was closely monitoring the Ethiopia program, a new agency appeared. Though I normally wouldn't have trusted a new agency, the lady who had begun this agency, Imagine Adoptions, originally called Kids-Link International, had another adoption agency called St. Anne's Adoption, which had programs in other countries and years of experience. St. Anne's had been around since the 1980s, which made me feel safe.

I had also heard rumors about the other agency that caused me to second-guess our initial decision to go through them. It wasn't anything unethical, but there were many complaints about their ever-lengthening wait times and lack of clear communication. Though I didn't know whether or not Imagine Adoptions would have those same issues, Imagine stood on a platform of putting the children first. They also released beautiful color newsletters showing the lovely facility that the children in Ethiopia would be staying in while they awaited their parents' arrival.

It was called their Transition Home. The babies were cared for in a loving environment with a small staff-to-child ratio. They were held and sung to and loved. The older children received instruction in English and, as it was a Christian agency, were taught about Jesus' love for them. They were fed nutritious meals, told about their adoption, and prepared for their new lives in Canada.

Parents picking up their children were welcome to walk through and see the other children and check out for themselves how great the home was. It all sounded wonderful. Because I knew myself and knew that for me, once we knew who our children were, it would be very difficult to trust them to be cared for by others, I chose the place where it sounded like they would be best looked after.

So it was that Mark and I decided to reapply to our province to work with the new agency.

When we initially did our home study for Ethiopia, we applied for a baby girl, as young as possible. At that point, my motivation was mostly about what I wanted and what I thought would be best for me. I investigated adoptive breastfeeding, bought a few little girl outfits, and dreamed of the day when my family would be complete—three boys and three girls, my six children, just as planned. Several times during the home study, the social worker asked if we were sure that we didn't want to consider adopting siblings, as she felt that we could cope with adding two more, given our fostering experience. We basically told her, "Thank you very much, but six kids will be plenty!"

International adoption required even more paperwork than we were used to with our other adoptions. It included items such as medicals and lab tests for us that required appointments. Having our fingerprints taken for our Interpol clearance was kind of fun, but photocopying and having reams of papers notarized was less amusing. We were able to cross off items on our checklist for our dossier (the large stack of required documents) through the spring and summer of 2007, and by fall we had our provincial approval and were waiting only for federal approval.

That's when I began to realize that God may have a different plan for our family than I did.

I had started reading *There Is No Me Without You*, by Melissa Fay Greene, an unwritten prerequisite for anyone considering adopting from Ethiopia. The tagline for the book, "One woman's odyssey to rescue her country's children," refers to the passionate mission of one woman named Haregewoin Teferra to save the lives of Ethiopian orphans and give them a future.

While I was reading this compelling book, even in the opening chapters before I really got into it, I began to think of our adoption differently. Part of the reason we had adopted in the past, and were adopting again, was to help children who needed a family to care for them, but our biggest reason, if I were to be honest with myself, was my desire to have another child. Reading the book opened my eyes to the plight of orphans elsewhere in the world, children who needed homes and didn't have a social system to fall back on. In Canada, if a child doesn't find an adoptive family, they may spend their childhood in foster homes or group homes. Although this isn't the life I would wish for any little one, it's one which ensures that a child will be fed, clothed, and have access to an education and medical care. In other parts of the world, there are no safety nets, no system to advocate for children's safety, nourishment, health, and education. A best case scenario in Ethiopia, for example, was for them to live in an orphanage, an institution that relies almost solely on donations and where food, education, and medical care may be sparse. These children die, and often they die alone.

As I read, my heart was opened to the suffering of children who were orphaned or abandoned and needed not only a family, but to have even their basic needs met.

Something shifted for me. I was reminded of all the verses in the Bible that call on us to care for orphans, and I knew that God had called me to do just that. I began redefining my motives and opening myself up to what God had in store for me.

I sensed very clearly that we were being called to adopt two children from Ethiopia, siblings, and that one was a boy and the other was a girl. I will admit to not being thrilled at first. I had wanted to be a mother of six kids, so seven didn't fit into my plan—or into my van! The very idea was overwhelming and scary. As I prayed about it, though, it became apparent that this might be God's plan for our family. I eventually came to a point where I was willing to move forward with it, except that I wasn't willing to tell Mark what I was thinking. It had taken a year before I had felt like Mark was fully on board with adding one more child, so I wasn't going to announce to him that I thought we were supposed to bring home two!

I didn't tell Mark anything, or even hint at the idea, but every morning in the shower I just prayed, "Okay God... you've got me convinced. Now, tell Mark."

Things continued to happen to point me in this direction, and I got to a point where I was positive that this was what God wanted for us. I knew that He had already chosen the children that were to be ours someday.

One morning, when I was in the shower praying, I very clearly saw a little boy's face. I could see him as plainly as if he were standing in front of me. I knew he was my son. He was older than I thought he would be. I had never imagined myself adopting a child older than a baby or toddler, but he was unmistakably there. Even though I had never been one for having prophetic visions, I never doubted after that day that this was our son.

By this time, I had finished reading the Melissa Greene book, and Mark was about midway through. He really enjoyed the information about Ethiopia's rich culture and history. He was annoyingly slow at getting through the book, though! We were on a flight when he finally finished the book, and that's when he decided that we should adopt siblings. He didn't mention it to me, however, because he knew how much my heart was set on a baby girl!

The next night, when all of the kids had finished eating their suppers and left the room, Mark commented to me that it would be nice for Josiah to have a younger brother, a boy closer to his age. He then asked me if I would ever consider adopting a child who was a little bit older, a boy perhaps.

I hid my smile and replied calmly that it was something I

would consider. We said nothing more on the subject that evening.

One or two days later, I was stirring dinner at the stove when Mark called me from Blockbuster to ask if there was a movie I would like him to rent for us. Then he asked if I had gone to the bank that day to get a draft to send to our adoption agency, so that our dossier could be sent to Ethiopia.

I told him that I hadn't—I was waiting to scc if we were going to make changes to our home study to ask for siblings, which would then require new approvals from our province and the federal government—but I didn't disclose my reasoning to him.

He then asked if the adoption fees were higher for adopting two. My heart was racing. I knew that God had orchestrated this and that Mark was open to adopting siblings.

I maintained the illusion of calm when I answered him. "There are no extra fees, but we would have to pay for another citizenship application, which is one hundred dollars. If they are over two years old, we would have to pay for another flight home. And, of course, there's the money to raise them to adulthood, but no, there are no extra adoption fees."

He took in my answer and then, to throw me off, asked me if it would be extra if we adopted three.

I laughed and told him that it would be very expensive, because he would then have to pay to send his wife to the loony bin! He laughed, too, changed the subject back to movies, and we said goodbye.

As soon as the call was over, I phoned my sister-in-law Deanne in B.C. She had been very supportive of this adoption, even planning to travel to Ethiopia with us. I had already told her about my belief that God's plans were for us to add two more children to our family, so I was bursting to talk to somebody. I couldn't conceive that Mark would even entertain this idea unless a miracle had occurred, so I had to share my excitement.

"I think Mark knows!" I told her.

That Friday, Mark and I sat across from each other in a restaurant at lunchtime on our wedding anniversary. We chatted about his work, and when there was a pause in the conversation he looked at me and said something along the lines of, "So if we were to get two, I was thinking that one would be a boy, about this old, and the other would be his sister, who would be younger than him." He then proceeded to give me the exact ages I had been imagining and talked about how much easier it would be for the two siblings to have each other. I was amazed that God had shown this plan to each of us separately.

We weren't naïve enough to believe that adoption was the answer to the myriad of problems facing children in developing countries, but we knew that it was something we could do. At the time, there were 5.3 million orphans in Ethiopia alone. A number that big is too much for our brains to even comprehend, and it often felt that giving a home to two of them was like trying to make a beach with just two grains of sand. However, we also knew that with God, those grains of sand could multiply. We had seen before that when adoption begins in a family, church, or community, its effects can be contagious. If no one else in a community has adopted, it is often too unknown, too frightening for people to consider, but if others have gone down that path and can share their experiences, others are more likely to follow. We also felt that by opening our eyes to the perplexity of the orphan crisis in Africa, we would be moved to help children in that continent in other ways, too, perhaps also influencing those around us.

I ordered thirty copies of Melissa Fay Greene's book and drafted a letter to accompany it. I wrote about how the book had impacted us without revealing our plan to adopt siblings. I asked people to read the book and to then pass it on to someone else. I also asked that they contact us when they finished reading so that we could share with them the decision we had been influenced to make.

I contacted our agency right away and we went about changing our paperwork. Mark wanted us to request siblings of any gender, but I couldn't let go of the idea that one was a boy and one was a girl, so when we initially applied for siblings, this is what we officially requested.

Many months later, I came to the very difficult decision that if we were going to trust God with this and let Him be in control, we needed to leave the details to Him. I shed some tears in the process of letting go of my dreams of adding another daughter to our family. I grieved my dreams of someday braiding her hair, scrapbooking alongside her, and watching her grow up with my other girls. It was a hard dream to let go of. Once I was able to relinquish that, Mark and I were both at peace with taking the specifications out and officially just requesting siblings of any gender combination. We looked forward to the future and seeing what God had in store for us.

I was still unsure of my ability to raise two more children in what was already a busy household, but when the doubts crept in I remembered that this was God's plan. I chose to trust Him to give me what I needed to parent all my children, the precious lives that He had entrusted to me.

Whenever the fears came, I would remember a specific quote which always brought me reassurance and comfort: "God does not call the qualified. He qualifies the called." Since I sure as heck didn't feel qualified, I leaned on Him to provide the needed strength, wisdom, and patience.

three

IN EARLY APRIL 2008, OUR DOSSIER ARRIVED IN ADDIS ABABA, THE CAPITAL city of Ethiopia. I had been given a tracking number by my caseworker at Imagine, Joanne, and I tracked its progress online as it made its way around the world, its contents set to change the makeup of our family. It was fun watching its stops around the globe to places I had never been, like New York City and Frankfurt, Germany. I was even able to see an electronic copy of the signature when it was picked up by an agency representative at its intended destination. It was exciting to be one step closer to our children!

Once your dossier is in Ethiopia, you are put in the queue to be matched with a child or a sibling group, depending on what you have been approved for. When you are matched with a child or children, it is called a referral. The timing of your referral depends not only on where you are on the list, but also on which family is felt would best suit a particular child. At the time we first applied, sibling referrals were taking three to five months. A few months into our official wait, this became twelve to sixteen months, with no certainties or ways to predict when our time would come.

Even after you receive a referral, the wait goes on. There is a court date—or, in most cases, several court dates—and once that is successful, months of additional waiting pass before Canada issues a visa for your children and you are allowed to go and pick them up.

The wait was intermittently unbearable, but there were enough moments of hopefulness to keep the expectancy alive. Some days I was obsessed with monitoring our progress, which was laughable because there was no real way to do this. None of the timing was in my control, so it was futile to pretend that any of it was! I checked the message boards, the adoption blogs, our agency's website, and my emails as though I were waiting on news that could change the outcome of the entire world.

In the first weeks, I felt sure that we would be one of the exceptions to the rule and that our referral would come at any moment, even though our file had only just arrived in Africa. As the weeks turned to months, my disappointment settled in and I slowly began to accept that the wait had only just begun.

The one bright spot in my seemingly endless venture of waiting was the new friendships I began to forge through meeting other adoptive or prospective adoptive parents online. I was kept sane by the message boards, blogs, private emails, and phone calls of others who were also waiting and those who had survived the wait and were now home with their children. From these people, those who knew how I felt because they had felt it, too, I received the encouragement, support, and information that allowed me to dream of the day when our turn would come.

Some days, I was consumed with thoughts about these children whom I had never met. I wondered how they were, and if at that moment they were in an orphanage or still with a family member. I worried about how they were feeling and whether or not they were hungry, sick, or scared. I prayed for them. I cried for them. I grieved for the losses they would endure. I loved the thought of them.

My thoughts often turned to their birth mother. I wondered if she was still living and what her life must be like. I couldn't

21

imagine being in a position where I wasn't able to meet the most basic needs of my children just because of the country I had been born into.

On Mother's Day 2008, I wrote these words,

> *Mother's Day has special meaning for me because I can't help but think of the other mothers without whom I wouldn't have some of my kids. This year, there is a mother on my heart who I have never met and who lives on the other side of the world…the mother of my future Ethiopian children.*
>
> *I have such conflicting emotions. On the one hand, I want a referral soon, but in order for that to happen, another mother's heart has to break. Right now, in a country far away, a mother is considering giving up her children to give them a chance at life.*
>
> *Perhaps she is widowed and cannot feed them. Perhaps she, too, is dying. Regardless of the circumstances, I know that this decision is the most difficult decision any person could ever have to make. I pray for this woman daily and wish there was another option for her and for her children, because as much as I want to be their mom, I am the second-best option for them.*

On the days when the wait felt never-ending, I reminded myself that the timing was ultimately up to God. I reassured myself with the knowledge that He had already chosen our children for us and us for them.

Many prospective adoptive parents had made themselves spreadsheets to track others' progress in order to watch themselves move up the "list." The list was really an imaginary thing, as our agency wouldn't release this information. In reality, the list was composed only of people who were online and who had shared the information about when their dossier had arrived in Ethiopia and what their child request was. There was a list for parents requesting infant girls, a list for those requesting infant boys, and a list for those requesting a baby of either gender. The list for those wanting to adopt an older child was shorter and the list for those wishing to adopt siblings was the shortest of all. Many of the waiting parents had printed color-coded spreadsheets and kept them up to date with precision. I jotted down those I knew of who had requested siblings ahead of us or just behind us in green crayon on a scrap paper. Later, when I had to add information, I did so using a pencil and some crudely drawn arrows. I scribbled the age range each family was open to accepting. I watched the progress of other families, crossing names off my list when they received their referrals, and celebrating the milestones along their journeys.

Through hearing or reading of their experiences, I was better able to visualize what it would be like when the day came for us to travel to bring our children home. I often had tears in my eyes when I read accounts of them being surrounded by a welcoming committee of friends and family at the airport upon their return. I was even able to take my kids and be there to help welcome a local family home with their two new daughters. In my mind, I could see the faces of our family and friends cheering us on someday when we walked through those doors, exhausted by travel but exhilarated to be home.

On the list of those waiting for siblings, there were three of us whose dossiers had arrived in Ethiopia within a month of each other. Ruth, Karen, and I had other things in common as well, like our faith, our love of blogging, and the fact that we were all homeschooling, so the three of us began corresponding on the computer, sharing tidbits of hope and information, offering moral support, and forming a friendship. Though our file had arrived first, Karen's referral was the first to happen of the three of us, as the age range she and her husband had specified was broader than ours. I was happy and felt encouraged for her, but I also felt a twinge of sadness. I had to rely again on my belief that God had a plan and that the two little girls who were referred to Karen were not meant to be ours.

Soon after Karen's referral in the spring of 2009, I called our caseworker to inquire about how things were looking and to ask if she had any idea when we might expect our big call. She was wonderfully sympathetic and sweet, but her gist was that the wait for siblings was continuing to get longer and that it looked unlikely that we would be bringing children home that year.

It was a letdown. I never imagined when we began the process two years earlier that we would have to wait so long without even seeing our children's faces or knowing who they were. Mark and I had been talking about the prospect of using our travel points to plan a family vacation, one last trip with the five kids before we brought home two more. After that phone call, we decided to make the trip a reality, so we booked a Disneyworld getaway for September 2009. We had done the math and knew that even if we did get a referral the next day, the visas required to bring the kids to Canada would not be ready before October at the earliest. We thought we were safe in booking the trip.

During our wait, we continued to form relationships with others who had adopted from Ethiopia and other parts of the world, both because it was a great source of support and because we felt it would be important for our children to someday know others who were also adopted or were from their birth country, who understood what it was like to be a black child being raised by white parents. We met others from our area, and even from other provinces, having barbeques, play dates, and even hosting a potluck for families who had adopted from Africa.

With three of our children being adopted, adoption was a topic that was spoken of freely in our home. We have been very open with our kids about their stories, in an age-appropriate way, and they do not feel that it is something to feel ashamed about. Instead, it's something to be celebrated. Josiah brought a book into his Sunday school classroom one day about Ethiopia and announced to his teacher (and anyone else in a five-mile radius) that his new brothers or sisters were going to have dark skin like him. We had all kinds of books on the subject of adoption, from picture books to chapter books, and it was common for it to come up in conversation—or even in play.

One day, I overheard my three little ones playing at the table with Barbie dolls. I couldn't help but eavesdrop and I had to hide my giggles at their sweetness:

BARBIE #1: "I have a baby in my tummy, but when it comes out I am not going to be able to take care of it."
BARBIE #2: "I will be the daddy that adopts the baby."
BARBIE #3: "I will be the mommy who adopts the baby. I will love the baby so much."
BARBIE #1: "Oh, the baby has been born. Baby, give your first mommy a kiss before you go live with your new mommy because she will miss you."

All of our other kids were getting swept up in the excitement of this adoption and wanting to know more about the birth country of their new siblings. The kids studied Africa in homeschool, their ears perking up at the mention of Ethiopia or Amharic, the language that their future siblings would speak. We took them to see the Ethiopia exhibit at Heritage Days, where they were captivated by the dancing. My brave ones tried traditional Ethiopian food served atop *injera*, a spongy flatbread used instead of utensils when eating. I got a glimpse that day of just how much our children were developing a genuine love for this faraway country.

One day, Mackenzie, our oldest, was watching the distance running in the Summer Olympics and he started to get really excited. He called me from the living room, saying, "You have to come see this. I think we're going to win all three medals!"

I thought something strange was going on, since Canada isn't exactly known for its impressive distance runners, so I came in to watch. It was then that I realized he was talking about Ethiopia. When the Ethiopian runners did come in first and second, Mackenzie felt as though "our" country had won!

I researched traveling in Ethiopia and relied on the experiences of others to start making lists of possible places to stay, eat at, or see. I looked into flights, even though it would be a long time before I could book them. My sister-in-law Deanne would come with us to volunteer where she could and to help us on the long flight home. We would also bring our oldest son, Mackenzie, as he would be old enough to appreciate the experience. I read travel books giving recommendations. I pored over people's pictures of the Transition Home, imagining myself meeting my children there. I hung on every word describing what many referred to as their "gotcha day," the day they finally met their child. Mostly, I just dreamed of the day when I would get to hold my new children in my arms so that I would have my own pictures and story.

As the months passed, I became more and more enamored with Ethiopia, and all of Africa. I read everything I could get my hands on and watched documentaries. I spoke to anyone who had visited or lived there. I met a new friend who had just moved to Canada from South Africa. My eyes were further opened to both the beauty and complexity of Africa through her stories.

As a family, we went to see the African Children's Choir and were buoyed by their enthusiasm and undeniable joy. Mark and I attended a dinner for Hope International. An Ethiopian man sitting at our table shared his own stories of growing up in the country we were eager to learn more about. He gave us his contact information at the end of the evening in case we wanted to get in touch with him before our travel to his birth country, as many of his family members still lived there. One thing was becoming clear the more I immersed myself in Africa once my eyes were opened: there would be no way for me to close them again.

I began to read not only of the diverse history of Africa and current beauty but also of its horrors. I read about the genocides in Darfur and Rwanda, of rape used as a weapon of war in the Congo, of child soldiers, female circumcision, forced marriage, and the persecution of Christians.

Mostly, I read of orphans. My heart cried out to help them. It seemed too tall a task. There were so many of them and only one of me. I was encouraged, though, by some of the stories I read of others who were making a difference. There were individuals who had started orphanages or hospitals, and organizations committed to bringing clean water to communities.

Change had begun, and I was intent to be a part of it.

four

It took us two years to save enough money for all the fees associated with international adoption. In order to save for the upcoming travel expenses in the depressed market, we began brainstorming fundraising ideas. Our most ambitious idea was to plan a dinner and silent auction, but we decided to put that on hold until we received our referral so that we would have pictures of our kids to add to the invitations. Plus, planning the event would help pass the many months between the referral and our travel. Given the timing of the bankruptcy, the dinner never took place.

Our first fundraiser was held at our house in November 2008. It was a bake sale, clothing sale, and book sale. My mom and I baked night and day for weeks, making more than two thousand baked goods. People were very generous and I was blown away by some of the acts of kindness we received. One lady, who was a stranger to me, donated a box of clothing. Some friends donated clothing and books, some baked, one helped the day of the sale, my friend Shannon came twice before the sale to help organize and price, others advertised it online and spread the word, and many made cash donations above what they bought.

We chose to split the proceeds of the fundraiser with Faya Orphanage in Ethiopia. We were so excited to send the orphanage a check for over $700, as well as to have a start to our adoption travel fund.

In the early spring of 2009, I took the clothing that had not sold at the earlier fundraiser to a one-day children's clothing sale. I printed off little signs explaining that the money was going towards our adoption. The response was incredible! It was lucky that Shannon, the same friend who had helped so much with the other sale, offered to come with me because there was a lineup the whole morning at our little table! I sold over $700 that day and went home exhausted, but very hopeful, about our growing fund. I sensed that since God was continuing to provide the money, perhaps our referral would come sooner than anticipated.

The idea to have a garage sale was born mainly out of my nesting. I had begun to feel that I needed to get the house prepared, and in doing so I had the desire to purge and declutter. Though I considered hanging on to some items such as clothing, coats, and shoes, we ultimately decided that it wouldn't be practical to save everything, since we didn't know if our referral would be for two boys, two girls, or one of each— nor did we know their ages or sizes.

Pretty much everything we could put a pricetag on went on sale. I went through every box, drawer, and closet in our house and garage, pricing and organizing. I sent out an email to our friends, family, and acquaintances asking for donations of items or help at the sale. Most importantly, I prayed that God's hand would be on this effort, that He would bring the items, bring the people, and give me the strength and energy to pull it off.

We decided to hold the sale at my mom's house, reasoning that more people would come if the sale were held in town as opposed to our acreage.

Even before the sale began, I was brought to tears by the generosity of others. My Auntie Judy offered to drive down from Calgary and help the night before, as well as the first day of the sale, which we expected to be the busiest. She made a seven-hour drive roundtrip just to be there for me. My mom took two days off her job, allowed us the use of her home and garage, and helped in so many ways, even insisting that the sale go on after her father passed away suddenly just days before the sale was scheduled to begin. I was amazed and humbled by how much we were blessed by people dropping off items or lending us their tables and clothing racks, or staying late into the night to help me price things and lay everything out. Large truckloads of stuff just continued to arrive.

Our kids were also fabulous. The little ones would run up to me with one of their toys saying, "You can sell this for my brothers or sisters." They seemed willing to sell it all. They were so sweet. Jonah spent hours and hours sorting through Lego and Playmobile, putting the sets into Ziploc bags. He agreed to work the concession stand with Mackenzie to raise additional funds. Mackenzie, who was fourteen at the time, even offered to spend his own money buying some of the food for the concession. While many teenagers were going through selfish phases, my older boys were giving freely of their time and money to help children to join our family. I was so proud of all my kids.

The night before the sale, we had so many items that they couldn't all fit into my mom's double-car garage. It was stuffed to the rafters when we closed that garage door. We knew that in order for anyone to even be able to step one foot inside, we were going to have to put more than half of the tables, large items, and boxes on the driveway and the front lawn. Unfortunately, the forecast for Thursday called for rain, all day. That night, I put it all in God's hands and put Him in charge of the details. When I took one last look at the mountain of belongings He had already provided, I had a feeling that He was going to bless us enormously. I went home for the night and slept soundly.

The morning of the sale, the clouds looked ominous as Mackenzie and I drove to my mom's house, but when we were in the middle of setting up, Mackenzie said, "Mom, look what God did!" I looked up and saw dark clouds all over the sky in every direction except for right above my mom's house, where it was clear and blue and beautiful! People started arriving before the official opening time, and from then until three days later, there was never a lull.

Many miracles happened during the sale, especially the first day. For the morning, the weather held and we were able to sell so much that when it started to sprinkle in the late afternoon, we had plenty of room to move everything inside the garage. When it did rain, it lasted only a few minutes.

I had advertised to local homeschoolers, because I was selling some of my homeschool curriculum. Many homeschool families came to the sale. In the afternoon of the first day, a van pulled up and the couple inside came over to have a look. When they saw the sign my brother Matt had made saying that the money was going towards our Ethiopian adoptions, they approached me and told me that they were just on their way to drop off some donations at the local charity store, but that I could have them if I wanted them. They weren't sure I would want them, though, because they were donating their old homeschool curriculum!

Two other strangers that first day also "just happened" to be on their way to the charity store with trunks stuffed full of toys, clothes, books, and puzzles… and they gave them to me for the sale, too. Another miracle was how much we sold. Tables and boxes that had been full were cleared right out! I had priced everything very cheaply, with around half of the items at ten cents each. My motto had become "getting to Ethiopia ten cents at a time." Some said not to bother with such a small amount, but dimes really add up when they are in God's hands!

My older boys had a great attitude about helping at their little concession table, never complaining about having to wake up early or about being bored. We put a large picture of our existing kids at the concession with the words, "Help us complete our family," and some customers insisted on paying for pops with twenty-dollar bills and didn't want any change.

It was a good opportunity for my boys to see the generosity of people in our community.

Periodically during the three days, friends would come with more boxes or entire truckloads of items to donate, so we had constantly changing inventory. Word of mouth spread about the best garage sale people had ever been to! Many of the same people came to the sale two or three times, because we kept getting new items. One evening, I looked around and the tables were almost empty. Though this was wonderful in one sense, we had advertised the sale to continue for one more day, so I was a bit worried about what we would have left to sell the last day. Right then, a van and a truck pulled up and two of my friends began to unload enough donations to fill many of the tables.

I was in awe of how God continued to work out the details. The people who came to shop at the garage sale were grateful that the prices were so low and they walked away happy, so we were able to bless others that way, too. It also seemed that some of the newcomers who came needed encouragement in their own adoption or homeschooling journey.

Many people said things to me such as, "I never go to garage sales and don't live near here, but today I happened to be driving in the area and I saw the signs. For some reason, I followed them and now I know why!" Many of those who stopped by expressed an interest in adopting and peppered me with questions about the different types of adoption. Since adoption is a topic that I'm passionate about, I was able to share my experiences and information. It was miraculous to see God woven throughout the sale in so many different ways, the largest being the amount of help I had. Some came for multiple "volunteer shifts." I couldn't have done it without so many helping hands and giving hearts.

I had already begun to think of this as "God's Garage Sale," but the total amount raised still astounded me, reminding me once again that with God, all things are possible. We raised just over $4,500 towards our trip to Ethiopia, a trip that was still some time off, since we had yet to receive our referral. We felt confident that with so many months remaining, we could acquire the rest of the money through a combination of saving and having our planned fundraiser dinner.

CHAPTER

five

THE GARAGE SALE TOOK PLACE IN EARLY MAY AND A FEW DAYS LATER, I TOOK the kids to my grandfather's funeral. Mark's work as a mortgage broker had been really busy, so both of us were at the point of exhaustion.

The buildup of stress started to take its toll, so we decided one day that we needed a little recharge. I suggested that we get away for a night to a hotel in Edmonton to leave all our worries behind, at least for a time, but my extremely spontaneous husband suggested that we instead pack everyone up and go somewhere, anywhere, where we could find a good deal on a place to stay.

A few hours and phone calls later, we had rearranged some scheduling details, packed for ourselves and the five kids, picked up Mark's laptop at his office, and were on the road to Canmore, Alberta. It was a very relaxing time. Mark got caught up on some work, the kids and I did a fair amount of homeschooling, we enjoyed swimming, and we did as much hiking as the cooler temperatures would allow.

That Tuesday, one of my sisters-in-law called my cell phone and asked if we had heard anything yet. It wasn't like her to ask, as she understood that it was difficult for us at times to always field questions about the adoption. However, she said that she had a strong feeling that our referral had come in. I told her that I didn't think there was any news, but that I would call home to get my messages and let her know if I learned anything. I called home with my stomach doing little flip-flops and was a little disappointed that none of our phone messages were adoption-related.

The next day, we were coming down a mountain after seeing a gorgeous waterfall, and laughing about Mackenzie and Jonah's attempt to scare me with their bravado near the edge of a cliff, when Mark got a call on his cell phone. I didn't think too much of it, given that this was, for him, a working vacation and he had already taken a call or two that morning.

He said a few things that sounded strange from his end of the conversation, however, so I asked him about the call when we got down to the van. He seemed to be acting oddly and he gave me an evasive answer, but I figured he would tell me at some point. I was so busy buckling the kids into carseats and ensuring that all their coats were accounted for that I almost forgot about the call.

When we got back to Canmore, Mark suggested that we go to a restaurant. After passing by several that were his type of eatery, he announced that today we should go to a fancier place. Mark didn't like going to nice restaurants when we had all the kids with us; he hated the scrutiny and the stares, as well as the pressure to keep them sitting properly and the fear that they would make a scene. I knew that something was up even before he stated, "We should go here because I have an announcement to make."

With that comment, I immediately thought of the suspicious call on the trail and wondered if we had sold a house. We had a rental property for sale and it seemed the only logical explanation. In my mind, this was the only possible impending announcement.

After we sat down in the steakhouse, Mark asked if I had a paper and a pen. I did not. He then took a business card out and used a brown crayon that the hostess had given the kids for their coloring sheets. He began writing on the back of the card. I assumed he was writing down a number and thought that for him to be making such a big deal of it, the house must have sold for *way* above list price.

Mark then held the card up for a minute and asked, "Are you ready to see something that will change your life?"

I honestly thought to myself, *This man doesn't know me very well if he thinks that any amount of money is going to change my life!*

He slid the card across the table with the writing facedown.

Nonchalantly, I flipped the card over. Reading those words did change my life!

WE GOT OUR REFERRAL.

I had to reread the card a second time and study the look on Mark's face before I believed that it was true.

So many emotions were wrapped up into one moment that it is difficult to explain how I felt. My first feeling was one of relief, because over the many months of waiting I had doubted if this moment would ever come, times when rumors circulated about the Ethiopian adoption program closing to large families or about the requirements changing. So, when I saw those words and knew that it was true, that we would be bringing children home, I felt immediate relief followed by joy, jubilation, excitement, and still a measure of disbelief.

My heart pounding, I asked Mark if they were boys or girls, and he said that he didn't know. He hadn't wanted to ask any questions on the trail because it would have aroused my suspicion as I walked next to him! I was trembling as I took his cell phone to call the social worker and ask for more details. She answered all of my questions and then promised to send the children's pictures to Mark's phone.

Immediately after hanging up with her, I announced to the kids that they would be getting a new brother and sister. They were all excited and peppered me with questions. As we were waiting what seemed like hours for the social worker to send the details and pictures to Mark's cell phone, I was shaking so much that the kids laughed at me. Mackenzie said, "Calm down and eat, Mom," referring to a lunch I don't remember tasting.

I was so excited to see my new children's faces, and yet so nervous at the same time. I wondered about what they had gone through in their lives up to that point and knew that from this moment forward our family would never be the same.

Finally, Mark got the email and opened it. He turned the phone around so that I could see a picture of our little boy and I completely lost it. It was the boy I had seen more than a year and a half earlier in my mind when I was praying about the adoption and asking for guidance. It was him! I didn't care that we were in public. I was shaking and crying and gushing over this sweet face. It astonished me how, in an instant, I knew that he would be ours.

When I saw the pictures of him and his little sister, there was this familiarity, this feeling that I had been waiting for them all along and that they just belonged in our family. It just felt *right*. While we were in the midst of the wait to end all waits, at times I felt like it would never happen, and now I felt so at peace with the timing. I knew that God had planned for us to have these particular two children, that the waiting was all a part of that, and it was worth every second of it.

I was astounded that the referral we received—one boy, one girl, the boy being older—was exactly the one we had planned for before deciding to leave the decision to God. I would have another daughter whose hair I could braid and who I could scrapbook with after all! We were thrilled! We were excited! We were nervous!

I asked Mark how he was feeling about this huge news and he said that it had taken awhile for it to sink in. At first, he'd felt nervous, but by the time he walked down the mountain, he had processed it and began to get excited. Seeing their pictures made it even more real for him.

Our kids were full of questions about their new siblings and glad that there would be both a new sister and a new brother. The little three discussed who would be sharing whose room and proudly announced what good big brothers and sisters they were going to be. Their biggest question was when they would get to meet them. The older kids were happy that there would be a brother and a sister and thought that their pictures were pretty cute. They also seemed relieved that neither of the kids would be in diapers, as was Mark. I had expected to feel a bit disappointed if our referral didn't include a baby. I'm a baby person and had secretly hoped for one last baby, but I was surprised to discover that once I saw my children's pictures, I felt only delight in exactly who God had chosen for us.

I called anyone whose phone number I could remember. I was bursting to share our news! Ironically, it took me about ten calls to finally reach someone who was home.

We took the kids on another little excursion to an old abandoned mining town in Banff National Park. While the kids explored with Mark, I mostly made calls. I couldn't wipe the smile off my face! It took me hours to reach Mark's sister Deanne, as she was out of the office for part of the afternoon, but she was so excited once I did get ahold of her and I promised to email her their pictures as soon as we got home. I was also anxious to get back to my computer so that I could share our announcement with the online adoption community that had been such a support to me over the years.

We had tickets to see a dinner theatre performance that evening in Canmore. During the show, I snuck out to the lobby to call and share the news with Shelley, a friend and neighbor who was also in the process of adopting. I wanted to get the phone number for the international adoption doctor in Edmonton, to get a consult. I had been telling complete strangers our news all afternoon, as I couldn't hold it in. The cashiers at the dinner theatre were no exception, so during the show they made a special announcement about our families' new additions and we got claps and cheers in response.

The rest of the show was mostly a blur, as I couldn't concentrate and was counting down the minutes until we could make our way back home. The minute the show was over, we piled into the van and cut our little vacation short to return to Edmonton.

We met with the social worker the next day.

After a referral, it is recommended that you consult with an international adoption doctor regarding the medical information before you make a decision. I phoned the office of Edmonton's Adoption Clinic and was told that the doctor was away for two weeks. On their recommendation, I phoned a doctor in Calgary. Over the phone, she discussed with me the heights and weights of the children who had been proposed to us. She also have me general information about some of the medical risks that children from Ethiopia may face, such as parasites, fungus, and the long-term effects of severe malnutrition.

The file attachment the social worker had sent regarding the children's medical reports hadn't been received, so the doctor recommended that I wait until she was able to review that information before we proceeded.

Even though we didn't yet have all the information, Mark and I discussed it and decided to go ahead and accept the referral. We both felt that God had chosen these two children for our family and that we should step out in faith.

I had some fears about the future. I had reservations about my abilities to meet all the needs of seven children. We had concerns about financing the trip. Mark felt the burden of providing for such a large family. I worried about attachment and about laundry. But the bottom line was that we had the chance to ensure that these two precious children of God would live.

We also knew the blessing that all children are and knew that they would add another dimension of love to our family.

We signed the acceptance papers on May 22, 2009. The little girl with the scared eyes and the little boy with the big grin were one step closer to being in our family.

CHAPTER

six

I WAS ON QUITE A HIGH AFTER FINALLY RECEIVING OUR REFERRAL. I PRINTED out multiple copies of the two pictures we had and posted them around the house. I gave them to anyone who would accept a copy and I emailed them to pretty much everyone else. I walked around with a permanent smile plastered on my face, my cheeks sore by day's end.

Just after we got the news, I went to a fundraising garage sale hosted by another adoptive mom and bought a shirt for our new son that had the word "loved" on it in Amharic. It was my first purchase for him and it made him seem more real. When I held the shirt, it was a tangible reminder that someday my little boy would be wearing it. My first purchase for my new daughter was also a shirt, one with the words "One cute Canadian." I thought of the day more than a year down the road when I would take her to our community's Canada Day festival, as one of the country's newest citizens. The worry, numbness, anger, sadness, hopelessness, jealousy, and fear that I had felt at times in the prior three years disappeared. The heaviness of the wait was gone in the instant that I saw the words "We got our referral."

Although we had finally received our referral, the adoption wouldn't be final until a successful court hearing in Ethiopia. In most cases, the first court date takes place months after the referral, and it can take three or more court dates before all the documents and witnesses are in place and the adoption can be granted, so we anticipated that it would be late in the year or early the following year before we would be able to meet our children. We were shocked to hear that our court date had already been scheduled and was set for June 22, one month to the day after our referral acceptance and the day of our son Jonah's twelfth birthday. I knew that this was a good sign, logical or not!

I had been told that on the day of your court date, if you pass, you get a phone call very early in the morning, because of the time difference. The night before, I took the phone to bed with me and didn't get much sleep when morning drew closer. Every time I looked at the clock and saw it getting later, I grew more and more nervous.

By 7:00 a.m., I crept down the stairs to check my computer. I had been told that if it was good news, it would be delivered by phone, but bad news would generally come by email. I was relieved to see that there was nothing from my agency in my inbox. I started drafting an email asking if they had heard anything about our court decision, but it sounded desperate no matter how I worded it, so I decided to just call.

My stomach was in knots as I dialed. Then, when I was put on hold for what felt like a very long time, it felt like there were hamsters running on wheels in my tummy. When the receptionist came back on the line to tell me that my caseworker wasn't at her desk, I tried to sound as casual as I could in leaving the message for her to return my call the second she got back!

Since no one else in the house was up, I got into the shower, keeping the phone next to the stall and not turning on the fan so that there would be no mistaking the ring. My breath caught when I finally heard the phone ring. With hair slick with unrinsed conditioner, I answered the call.

When my caseworker asked how I was, I muttered, "Um, okay," and then politely asked how she was. What I was really thinking was, *You tell me how I am. If we passed, then I'm great. If we didn't, then I stink.*

"I'm very good," she said, "and I think you will be, too, when I tell you that you passed court. You are now legally their parents!"

With only a towel wrapped around myself, I went into our bedroom to wake Mark with the news. I still felt shocked, but relief and happiness were beginning to sink in. Still wearing my towel, I went downstairs to announce the news to our online adoption community and to call Deanne, my mom, Mark's parents, and a few other friends and family. It wasn't until about an hour later that I finally finished my shower and got the conditioner rinsed out of my hair!

Once the news had settled in that I was now legally the mother of seven children, though somewhat anxious, I was mostly overcome with joy. June 22, 2009, was also the day that we received updated pictures of the kids. I stared into the eyes of our new son Elijah and wished that I could know more about him; I wondered how he would react to all the changes that were in store for him. I looked into the face of my new daughter Sedaya for clues about her personality and her past. I was sad for all that they had lost, and would continue to lose, in order to gain a family, but I was so happy that they would always have each other.

The day that we passed court, my friend Justine arrived from B.C. with seven of her kids. I would later realize that the timing of her visit was God's, as it helped prepare me for what was to come. I was able to see her girls, who had been home from Ethiopia for only ten months, and observe how well they were adjusting. I marveled at how quickly they had learned the language. This gave me reassurance that could only have come from seeing their progress myself.

Justine brought along some donations of clothes and shoes for me to take to Ethiopia, and some medicine that was left over from her trip. She taught me some tricks for caring for and styling her girls' hair. While it was fresh in my mind, I ordered all the hair products I would need for Sedaya. Justine also gently pointed out that it may be a good time for me to get better at delegating some of the housework and involving my kids more in these tasks.

After spending time with one of Justine's oldest boys and hearing about all the chores he was responsible for at his house, Mackenzie offered to start doing his own laundry. Not having the burden of all the housework, cooking, and laundry would be a blessing in the future.

While Justine was in town, we also decided to have a small get-together with other Ethiopian adoptive families. That evening, over supper, four moms discussed hair care, parasites, language acquisition, and where to purchase traditional Ethiopian food locally. At the time, I thought I was tucking the information away for a time half a year later when I would need it.

By the morning, when we waved off Justine and her brood, I felt more confident about my ability to parent another two children, and I'd gleaned some insider information about the adoption of older children from her and the other ladies.

Another adoptive mom, who had just returned from picking up her child in Ethiopia, took the time to speak to me by phone and I took some notes during our call that later proved invaluable. She had all sorts of tips for traveling with a scared child who doesn't speak the same language and she emailed me a page of common Amharic words, as well as the packing list she used. I was so grateful to get her packing list, as I had found many lists online pertaining to the adoption of babies but none for older children. I had no idea where to even begin, so her list gave me a starting point.

She also told me that the best thing they had purchased turned out to be a Cabbage Patch doll and extra outfits they had brought along. The next day, I took all the kids to Toys "R" Us and picked out a Cabbage Patch doll for Sedaya and ordered some extra doll clothing on EBay. I didn't find anything that day for Elijah, but I wasn't concerned in the least as I had months and months to find something special for him.

A strange occurrence began to happen shortly after we received our referral. I began to always feel like I was missing something. It was as if my brain knew that two of our kids were in Ethiopia, but there were still seven kids in my heart. At the farmer's market one evening, for example, I was doing a mental check to see that all the kids were accounted for. I could clearly see that Josiah was over at a booth with Mackenzie, Jonah was walking in front of me, and Gracelyn and Eliana were right beside me, holding my hands. Yet I felt almost panicky, like they weren't all there. I had to rescan and recount a number of times.

When I had them all in the van to go home, it happened again. In my rearview mirror, it looked like I was missing someone, so I turned around and looked only to see that everyone was in their carseat or seatbelt. I still felt off, so I checked to see that I had my purse and my purchases from the market, but I still felt the strange absence of something.

Then it occurred to me that it was my two in Ethiopia who were missing. Once I realized what it was, I was fine. I felt ridiculous and had to laugh at myself! It was also weird to answer the question of "How many kids do you have?" as it felt like I had seven, even though two were still in Africa. In a way, our lives were in limbo.

On July 1, 2009, Canada Day, we stood outside in our yard and took family pictures to send to Elijah and Sedaya. Mark and the boys were all wearing navy shirts with a Canada flag on them, the same one that we were including in the package for Elijah so that he would know that he was now part of our family. Our girls wore special dresses bought just for the photo; another matching dress for Sedaya would be making its way along with the photo albums.

It was exciting to pack up their little gifts and know that the next person to hold these items would be my children. We were only allowed to send a Ziploc bag for each of the kids, so I carefully chose everything to be included. In each of their bags, we included a stuffed toy/blanket and we all took turns sleeping with them for a night before we sent them off so that they would carry our scent. It was a way of including our other kids.

Just before I sealed up the bags, the kids and I gathered in the kitchen and gave a hug and a kiss to the stuffies and prayed together for their new brother and sister. It was fun to imagine them opening their bags filled with photos, toys, clothes, trinkets, and stickers. I wondered what they would think of our pictures when they saw them. Would they wish for a mom who was taller or prettier, or would they just be glad she was smiling? Would they be happy to know that they would have so many new brothers and sisters, or would they wish they were coming to a family where they would be the only children? Would they notice that my hair was black and curly like theirs, or would they only see that my skin color was different?

With excitement and hesitation, I shipped off those bags. I knew that when the bags arrived, our kids would be told about us and about the plan for them to come to Canada. On the day they opened their care packages, pictures would be taken of them wearing their new clothes and looking at our photos. These pictures would then be sent to us. Would I be able to see Elijah and Sedaya's reactions in the pictures?

It was too early to start packing with our trip so many months away, but I began to get organized by making lists. I'm not by nature a very organized person. Our home can at best be described as organized chaos, but I had come to the realization that things went more smoothly when I had at least *some* systems in place. I made a plan for creating freezer meals and worked out a schedule so that if I started making the freezer meals in mid-August, I would be able to have enough made to last three or four months after we returned home. I also made lists of items that needed to be purchased, such as clothing, sheets, pillows, medicine, and donations to bring on the trip. We began saving money for the new beds we would have to buy and I purchased dressers for Elijah and Sedaya, though the drawers remained empty. We planned out how much we would have to set aside each month in order to save enough for the trip's expenses. I booked the first appointment for our travel immunizations, feeling that as long as I managed to stay organized, I might just be ready by the time November came.

seven

ON JULY 13, THE FATEFUL DAY OF IMAGINE ADOPTION'S BANKRUPTCY, AS WE were driving home from Banff, my first action call was to Shelley. Shelley and I had gone to high school together, although we shared none of the same classes and were in different social circles at the time. She had contacted me through Facebook about two years earlier, having heard via the grapevine that we were adopting from Ethiopia. She and her husband were interested in adopting from there as well and were looking for information.

I am a huge advocate of adoption in general and was so excited that they were considering it. I encouraged her in their considerations, and even recommended Imagine Adoptions to them. They had applied to adopt some time after us and received their referral for a baby boy the previous Christmas. Their wait had been agonizing; they had already waited over five months to pass court and were still waiting for Canadian Immigration to process a visa so that they could go and pick up their son. It was estimated that their visa would come in August, so their excitement had built considerably now that they were on the home stretch.

The bankruptcy changed everything instantly. The news turned their world upside-down. Over the months, Shelley and I had gotten to know each other and had celebrated for each other when there was progress in our adoptions. We also vented to each other when we hit rough patches. My call to her confirmed what we now believed to be true. Imagine Adoptions had gone bankrupt.

Her information came from sources I thought were quite reliable. Since I had no access to a computer, she read to me some of the posts on the adoption message board that had first sparked the rumors that morning. Several adoptive parents who had received their visas and were in Ethiopia to pick up their children were urging any parents who had already passed court to get on an airplane and come. They had been told by employees at the Transition Home that the money was gone, food was running out, and there had been no contact from the agency in Canada to tell them what to do. There was no longer even money for gas to take the kids for the medical appointments required for permanent resident visas. They felt that the children were in immediate danger. The parents on the ground described chaos and fear.

Shelley was as upset as I was, but her tears were determined. She was going to get her son home safely. She gave me the phone number for our Member of Parliament. She had already been in contact with the MP's office, and they were expecting my call; she had told them that another family in their riding was caught up in this mess. I added the number and the contact name to my little notepad. Shelley understood how important information was, so as we hung up she promised to stay in contact and let me know the second she heard anything new.

After relaying to Mark what Shelley had said, I called the MP's office and spoke to a woman named Lottie. I didn't know it at the time, but I was to speak with Lottie every day over the coming weeks; her compassion, along with the efforts of Leon Benoit, our MP, would become invaluable in our efforts to get our children home.

Lottie listened to me for a few minutes and was sympathetic to our situation. Their office would help in whatever way they could. In order to inquire about the status of our children's visas on our behalf, she would need information about our kids, information that I did not have with me in the vehicle on the way home from our little Banff getaway. I jotted down what she needed and made plans to get back to her once I had the proper documents in hand.

Lottie had already begun to make inquiries about Shelley's son's file and had yet to hear back, but said that if she heard anything about the plan for the files of kids affected in the bankruptcy, she would let me know right away. I exchanged email and phone numbers with her and asked about protocol for getting emergency visas issued. She promised to look into the possibility.

It was in the times of idleness, the times when I wasn't on the phone gathering or giving information, that the worry crept in and overtook me and the tears flowed. Our trip home seemed to take forever. The weather had turned and, with the rain pounding on the windshield, it was difficult to see, forcing Mark to slow right down. Home and my computer seem further and further away.

Somewhere near Airdrie, the traffic came to a complete halt and we were stuck for twenty minutes or more in almost the same spot, only occasionally being able to inch forward. I felt such an urgency to get home, yet the drive would stretch to be an additional two hours because of the weather and construction delays. It felt like it took an extra two weeks.

Mark, at least, was thinking clearly. As he spoke, it became clear how much we would have to do to prepare for him to leave for Ethiopia for an indeterminate length of time. He began to think of the practical things that needed to be done and asked me to make some phone calls for him. We called his lawyer and begged to get us in as soon as possible in order for Mark to sign over Power of Attorney to me in case anything happened while he was away that required his signature, thus ensuring that we could still complete a real estate sale that was scheduled for the following week.

I remembered that our first of three appointments for travel immunizations was already scheduled for the following afternoon. We worked our other appointments around that one, thinking that one round of shots would offer more protection than none.

Our three youngest kids happened to be registered in a week-long Bible day camp that week. I had planned on rescheduling them to a different week, as they would already be missing the Monday while we made our way back from Banff, thinking it would be more worthwhile for them to go during a week when they could attend all five days. However, in my harried state the week before Banff, I had forgotten to make the phone call. That would prove to be a huge blessing, as we essentially did not have to worry about childcare for the youngest three children for the next four days.

I called my friend Diane Carpenter, whose two sons were friends with our older boys and who had been so supportive and helpful with our plans for this adoption, and let her know what was going on. I asked her if she could take our older boys the next day. She offered to keep them for the next few days, an offer that I at first did not think would be necessary but was thankful for. I also dialed someone from Mark's office and he spoke to them about the possibility that he may be gone for many months. Mark made other business-related calls and knew that getting his business affairs in order would be a huge task. When we couldn't think of any other productive things to do, we listened to an Amharic language CD and, with foggy brains, tried to absorb as much as we could, knowing that we would need the knowledge far sooner than expected.

The CD, Simple Amharic for Adoptive Families, had arrived in the mail shortly before the weekend and I had grabbed it at the last minute in case we had the opportunity to listen to it a few times in the van. Four days earlier, we'd made a nine-hour drive to pick up Mackenzie at camp in the opposite direction before heading to Banff, and we had played the CD two or three times. We had joked about it being lucky that we still had many months to learn some of the basics as we botched attempts to imitate what we were hearing. Upon arriving in Banff, we had only managed to memorize the Amharic phrase for "I love you."

Both Mark and I called in favors on that drive wherever we could get them, and tried not to think about the scary things, like Mark being gone for many months, me having to care for the five kids by myself, how in the world we would pay for any of it, and the scariest of all—what he would find when he got to Ethiopia.

Were our kids okay?

Arriving home from Banff, I headed straight in to the computer room and checked my email. One of the first messages I got was one that had been sent on Friday, July 10, by my caseworker at Imagine. The tone was cheerful and the message read:

> *Mark and Sharla,*
> *Hope this finds you well. Just wanted to let you know we received your gift packages today and they were sent via DHL to our fostering home this afternoon. Will forward your pictures once we receive. Have a wonderful weekend.*

It was bizarre to be reading it after all that had happened, to know that she'd had no indication of a problem on the last business day before the bottom fell out. I later found out that the employees had worked as usual that Friday until sometime in the afternoon, when it was announced that this was their last day of work. At that point, they were not allowed to contact any of their clients.

One of the blessings that immediately became apparent was that we had copies of all the documents necessary for our kids' visas. After the court process was complete, court documents were provided and translated, and new passports and birth certificates were issued, requiring the children to be taken for pictures. Although all the documents could normally take a month or more to obtain, we received copies of everything two weeks after our court date, and were told that all of the originals had been couriered to Nairobi, in Kenya, where the Canadian High Commission was located. We were told when we received the documents to expect the visas to be issued sixteen to twenty weeks later, so we expected to be traveling in early November.

That first night of the bankruptcy, I printed out copies of all the documents and began to add information to my notebook. I wrote down the ID numbers our kids had been given and their legal birthdates, as well as any other information that I thought might be asked for when I made inquiries the following day. Mark had somehow managed to get the other kids and bags in from the van and was starting to get the kids ready for bed.

Once they were tucked in, I packed their bags for day camp the next morning and returned a few phone calls. One of the calls I made was to my online friend Karen, whose two daughters were in the Transition Home with my kids. Though Karen and her husband had received their referral almost a month before we had received ours, the court date making the girls theirs had only happened twelve days prior and they had not yet received copies of their documents.

Karen and I compared information. What little either of us had was sketchy at best, but I took comfort in talking to someone else who was in our situation. She and her husband had decided to stay put for the time being until they could determine what would be done to get visas without the required documents, or until they could track down the documents. Karen and I would later learn that her girls and my kids were originally from the same orphanage, had come from the same village, and had been close family friends! What a blessing for the four kids to be adopted by families who knew each other and who could allow them to stay in contact even once they were in Canada!

On the long drive that day, when I wasn't thinking about our kids, I thought about the families who had been waiting for referrals, whose hopes of adding a child to their home had been shattered. I thought mostly of my friend Ruth, and some of the tears I cried that day were for her. I sent her an email that night, but the intense weight of the implications of the day's events for Ruth and her family was unfathomable. I typed out, "I have thought of you so many times today, and every time I did, I couldn't stop the tears. There are just no words. I'm so sorry."

Ruth and her husband had waited longer than I had for this adoption and were next in line for older siblings. I didn't know what to say to her and my heart ached not only for them, but also for the two precious Ethiopian children who might never get to be part of their loving family.

That night, the hours after it was too late to make calls were the most difficult. I had done as much as I could to prepare for the battle that awaited us the following day and was left with the silence of the house and the fears that came in that silence. My body felt physically ill every time I allowed my mind to think about my kids being in a third-world country without access to medical care and not enough food. Here I was, in my cozy house with cupboards full of provisions, yet I was helpless to protect them.

I cried. I prayed. I cried some more. I tried to sleep and was only able to get in a few short naps. In between, I came down and checked the message boards, blogs, and forums, hoping that someone would have some new information. What I most craved was a report from someone who was there, someone who could tell me that they had seen my kids and that they were okay.

CHAPTER

eight

AS SOON AS THE LIGHT STARTED FILTERING IN THE NEXT MORNING, I BEGAN the day with determination and purpose. I now had lists of tasks to accomplish and a list of items to purchase. I had contact numbers of people to call who might be able to help us, and I had important facts to give them. I had a few hours of sleep behind me and a narrow window of time to be productive while my younger kids were at day camp.

Mark had arrangements to make with regards to his work and he and I made plans to stay in contact, as we would have to meet up later in the day for our shared appointments. It felt good to have a plan. On the drive to drop the kids off, I called our MP's office and left a message for Lottie with my cell number. Once I had the kids signed in and settled, my phone rang and as I answered it, I hurried to my van to access my notebook. I was able to give Lottie all the information I had pertaining to our Ethiopian kids and she was able to update me on their office's efforts to make inquiries on behalf of our and Shelley's family. With the information that I had given her, she planned to contact the High Commission in Nairobi and query the status of the visa applications for our children. The biggest concern in our case was finding out where our documents were and ensuring that they arrived in the proper hands in Nairobi.

I called Shelley and she kindly agreed to keep me updated during the course of the day of any new developments that came to light online, as I would not have access to a computer until the evening. I returned the call of a local adoptive mom who had brought home her girls the year before with CAFAC, the other adoption agency we had considered working with. She expressed her concern and offered to drop off some clothing her girls had outgrown. She also asked if I was interested in being interviewed for a news story, as her husband worked for the CBC. This was the first time I considered that the media would be interested in the story. I dismissed the idea quickly. The thought was so far out of my norm that it only added to my feelings of bewilderment. I had already stepped outside my comfort zone that morning in speaking to a government office, and publicity wasn't something I welcomed in that moment.

In the melee of calls, it was suggested that I call my cousin Don Guenette, who was involved in politics in his small town and had a friend in federal politics. I left a message on his voicemail, then went into a children's clothing store to begin shopping for the many articles of clothing we needed.

I had purposely not begun to shop for clothes, since we were supposed to be getting monthly updates on our kids, including new heights and weights. I know how quickly kids can grow at that age, so it would have been pointless to buy anything until closer to our travel date. We were also supposed to receive tracing outlines of their feet in order for us to determine their shoe size, but I would now have to buy multiple sizes for each and hope that something would fit.

As it was an outlet store, I found good deals on coats, shirts, and pants, but I couldn't decide on anything. I would pick things up and my heart would race. Just holding these items in my hands brought so many questions to mind about my kids and how they were doing. I started to get sweaty and felt shivers coming on. It felt as if I might panic right there in the store, in front of the other shoppers and staff.

When trying to decide on a coat for Elijah, I felt the tears come. What color would he like best? What size would he be when we arrived? Was the height and weight we had gotten for him a month earlier accurate, or had he already begun to lose weight from lack of food at the place we had trusted to care for him?

I put down the coat and walked out of the store empty-handed. It felt as if I was going to lose control there in the parking lot, when the vibration of my cell phone saved me from another meltdown. It was my cousin Don, and the care in his voice brought me back from complete despair.

Don expressed his sorrow over the situation and said that if we would send him an email explaining what we knew and giving any helpful information, he would send it to his friend at the Parliament and they would get to the bottom of it.

I took down Don's email address in my ever-growing notebook and called Mark to arrange to come to his office so I could use his computer. When I arrived at Mark's office, he and I drafted a letter to Don. We were sure to include things that, although they would be obvious to Don, would be valuable for his parliamentary friend to be able to get the whole picture of how Mark's absence would affect our family, if it were to be for an extended period. We also included the fact that we had five other children at home and that Mark was self-employed and our only source of income. We included the file numbers that we had been given for our kids. With a small glimmer of hope, we clicked "send."

While at Mark's office, we printed out color copies of all the documents we had received pertaining to the kids and placed them in a folder, in case Mark would need to travel to Nairobi with the documents. We knew that color copies probably wouldn't be sufficient, but they were the best option we had. There were so many unknowns, but we wanted to be prepared for any possible scenario.

Lottie called to let me know that she had been in touch with the Canadian High Commission in Nairobi and had given them our information. She said that, unfortunately, they did not have any record of having received our documents and could not proceed without them. I had no idea where to start in terms of locating the original documents, but I had to find them in order to get our kids home. My best chance was to find a way to get in contact with someone at the Transition Home in Ethiopia. This was daunting, because no one had any contact information for the staff there.

Mark and I drove together from his office to our appointment downtown for our travel immunizations. I'm not sure the nurse knew what to make of it when we told her that Mark would be traveling to Ethiopia within the week and staying an indefinite period of time. We also weren't sure at that time if Mark would have to travel in person to Nairobi, so we needed to be sure that he was covered for any shots he may need for that area, too. We weren't sure if I would be meeting him in Africa, as it would depend how long our kids' visas would take, but we wanted to make sure that I was covered, just in case.

We made sure to get prescriptions for an antibiotic, just in case we got sick while over there. I got my shots first, then went into the hallway to return more calls while Mark had his needles administered. The calls gave me no new information, but did add more in the way of rumors and speculation. For example, there was new information revealing that the executive director of Imagine Adoptions, Sue Hayhow, was being criminally investigated by the Cambridge Police Department, along with her business partner Andrew Morrow. The two were alleged to have embezzled hundreds of thousands of dollars from the agency. There was another rumor circulating that the two of them had been carrying on an affair with each other, although both were married to other people. This rumor did prove to be true.

It seemed that a moral fade had begun with the affair and the slip in integrity became steeper and steeper. They had both apparently arrived in Ethiopia the day before and given a small amount of money to provide eight days of food for the children at the Transition Home, though this was all from second- and third-hand sources. I supposed that if the rumors about the fraud and embezzlement were true, the least they could do was give up some of their stolen money to feed the orphans that they had caused to go hungry for many weeks! From the travel clinic, Mark and I drove to the lawyer's office.

On our way home, we were mostly silent, listening to the Amharic CD, unable to absorb any of the foreign words we were trying to learn. We headed straight to the church where the kids were, picked them up, and then later transferred them to my van. I picked something up for them to eat on the way home and Mark stayed late at his office. I gave no thought to not having eaten that day, as I still wasn't hungry. Just feeding my other kids caused me to struggle with the guilt of not being able to feed Elijah and Sedaya. I didn't even know whether they had eaten that day or not. I tried to push those kinds of thoughts out of my head, but they fought their way back time and time again.

With the kids in bed, I began to read up on the citizenship and immigration process, in hopes of arming myself with information for what might lay ahead. Many months earlier, before we had ever heard of Elijah and Sedaya, we had been given the choice of bringing home our future children either by permanent resident visa or by citizenship. The permanent resident visa had been the only option to parents adopting children overseas until less than two years earlier when, adoptive families had won the right to bring their children home as citizens. Most parents were still choosing to go with the tried and true option of permanent resident visas, because its timelines and process were fairly predictable. However, Mark had decided that we should go the citizenship route. He liked the fact that we would immediately be able to apply for Canadian passports for our kids upon arrival in Canada, and therefore could travel elsewhere with them. I thought the likelihood of us taking seven children to the United States, or anywhere else that required planes and packing, during our first year home was lower than us flying naked to the moon, but I agreed since I liked the idea of less paperwork.

The timelines for citizenship were much less predictable and had been steadily climbing in the weeks before this fiasco, but this choice turned out to be another blessing, another example of God's protection for our family. When bringing home kids under a permanent resident visa, an additional medical is required. As the Transition Home in Ethiopia had run out of funds, there was no gas money to take the kids to these medical appointments. Therefore, the kids caught up in the bankruptcy who were coming home under the PRV system were much further behind in terms of having the necessary paperwork for their visas. Waiting children whose adoptive parents had applied for citizenship were able to skip this step. What had originally looked like a gamble now turned out to save us additional time and stress in the quest to get our kids home safely.

After boning up on my citizenship and immigration knowledge, I ventured over to the adoption message boards only to be hit by more rumors. Fear struck hard and heavy. The newest speculations were varied, but if well-founded, they were terrifying. One was that the Ethiopian government might overturn the adoptions if they suspected anything unethical with our now-defunct agency and that the legality of the adoption orders were in jeopardy. Another was that as none of the caregivers had been paid at the Transition Home for close to two months, all of the kids were possibly to be returned to their original orphanages. The latter had a ring of truth to it, as we had already been told by a credible source that any children at the Transition Home who hadn't yet been referred were in the process of being transferred back to their originating orphanages.

I was scared, because I knew only the name of the orphanage our kids had come from and that it was located in an outlying village. I knew that all orphanages in the region were overcrowded as it was and that my kids must surely be scared enough without having to endure another move. My biggest fear was that if my kids were transferred elsewhere, we would lose track of them. They were in a foreign country that functions very differently than ours, so finding someone would prove almost impossible if you couldn't pinpoint a location. I sent a message asking anyone who knew the location of the orphanage our kids had come from to please contact me. The responses I received were mostly from other frantic parents whose children were also from that orphanage. The name of the village it was located in was the closest I could come to ascertaining a location.

Sometimes the fears threatened to paralyze me, but I pushed through. At these times, I often tried to turn to prayer but the words usually didn't come. I took comfort in knowing that God knew what the desires of my heart were and I reminded myself hourly that He loved these kids much more than we ever could, and that though they couldn't be in my hands, they were in His.

Another thing I discovered that night was that the Ministry of Women's Affairs in Ethiopia, commonly referred to as MOWA, was closed for two weeks for training. It remained to be seen if this was something that worked in our favor or not, as MOWA was in charge of all things related to adoption in Ethiopia and it was my understanding that they would have had the power to overturn the adoptions if they had any concerns, and/or to move the children back to their originating orphanages. However, MOWA would also have had the authority to step in and assure that the kids in Imagine's Transition Home were being cared for and fed. From the little I knew of MOWA, their first priority was always the children. We will never know if things would have been different had MOWA not been closed during the height of this bankruptcy scandal, but it did add another layer of uncertainty at the time.

Some parents had decided to sign Power of Attorney over to other families who were traveling to Ethiopia immediately.

They reasoned that if the Transition Home were to close, then those parents would be able to take custody of their children until they could get there themselves. It amazed me that even under the extreme stress of the moment, people who had been strangers just days earlier were coming together to share ideas, trust each other, and help each other.

Just after midnight, I pulled the suitcases out of the storage room and began packing for Mark. He had not yet returned from the office and I knew that sleep would be impossible with all the worry, so I began to pack. As I filled the suitcase with folded underwear and socks, I broke down in tears again, faced with the reality that I wouldn't be there to meet the kids together with Mark. I had dreamed of that moment for three years and the thought of missing it was agony. I had many selfish reasons for wanting to be there. I wanted to see the birth country of my children and to get to know them away from the chaos of our busy household. However, the reason that tore at my heart had nothing to do with me. I had heard from other adoptive parents who had sent only one spouse to pick up the kids that it often came to light months or even years later that the child had felt unwanted by the parent who hadn't come to Ethiopia to retrieve them. With all the emotion surrounding the changes that come from moving to a new country and new family, I didn't want to risk added feelings of insecurity and rejection to my children's tender hearts.

I had no idea in that moment, crouching on my bedroom floor and folding Mark's clothes, how I would manage to get to Ethiopia in these circumstances. I just knew that I had to try.

nine

JULY 15 WAS A WEDNESDAY. IT DIDN'T SEEM POSSIBLE THAT ONLY TWO DAYS earlier, we had been in Banff, enjoying a nice holiday, oblivious to the plight of our children half a world away.

When I was sure she would be awake, I gave Shelley a call. Neither of us had anything new to report, but, in the midst of the chaos, talking to someone else who understood what this felt like was akin to drinking warm tea, soothing and peaceful. On this day, there was a buzz of anticipation in the air, as it had been stated on Wednesday that Imagine Adoptions would be making a public statement. We felt sure that the statement would include an announcement specific to the children in the Transition Home. We hoped we would finally get answers about the future of our children and be told what our next steps should be. Shelley and I were both surprised that there hadn't been any news yet, as Imagine was located in Ontario, in a time zone several hours ahead of us.

A short time later, I received an email from Shelley that offered new hope. She had used her excellent detective skills to figure out the email address of the main contact at the Transition Home in Ethiopia, and she had received a response. It was a small, unexpected miracle and she shared the contact information with me. I had butterflies of excitement, not ones of fear, as I emailed a short query to the woman named Mary*, introducing myself and inquiring about our kids and their missing documents.

It was still very early in the morning, which meant that it was late afternoon in Ethiopia, and I was eager to see if she would reply. If she did, we might learn the status of the all-important documents. Less than half an hour later, Mary responded! She informed me that our kids' documents had been sent out on July 6 through DHL and gave me a tracking number for them. She also wrote four words which made my spirits soar with renewed hope: "The kids are fine."

Though I had no way of knowing if those words were an accurate depiction of the condition of my children, I chose to allow a moment of relief to sink in before I checked the DHL website. Holding my breath as I typed in the tracking number, my momentary relief was soon replaced with disappointment when the website relayed that I had entered an invalid number. I tried calling DHL, but was put on hold. Since I had to get the kids ready for their day, I took down the number in my notebook to call later.

Mackenzie and Jonah were still at my friend Diane's house, but I needed to take the younger three to their day camp again. While beginning to get them ready for their day, I received a phone call from someone at the offices of Alberta Children's Services. I whispered for the kids to finish getting dressed and went into another room to speak with her.

The woman I spoke to was so compassionate and empathetic. Her tone immediately put me at ease. She was genuinely sad for us and for what all the families involved were going through. When my voice choked up speaking about our concern for our children, she cried, too. This was another reminder that, although this was might have all been happening by the evil of one or two, there was so much goodness in humanity—in people.

I added her information to my notebook and glanced at the clock, realizing that I had to get going. I managed to get the kids and their bags (with sunhats, EpiPens, and water bottles) into the van, but I had no time to pack their lunches. I stopped at a convenience store and bought them some semi-healthy food, but before I could think of buying anything for myself, my cell phone rang again and I quickly paid for their lunches and took the call. Disappointingly, it was another adoptive mom who had nothing new to report.

I called DHL. After holding for a long time, I was put through to someone who informed me that I had a tracking number that didn't exist. I was crushed. I explained the situation to him and pleaded with him to search their records for something that had been sent from Addis Ababa by Mary on July 6. He wouldn't give me the information, as I wasn't the one who had sent the package. The day had started with such promise, but now I was at another dead-end.

I got the kids settled in their day camp. As I was getting back into my van, Lottie from the MP's office called. She had good news. She had been in touch with the High Commission in Nairobi and the staff there was aware of the extreme circumstances and would be giving our files priority. There was a good chance that we would be able to get expedited visas for our kids if they could locate our documents. This, of course, was the bad news. Even after direct contact with the Transition Home, the documents were no closer to being found than they had been the day before.

I drove to a nearby mall. I found myself again unable to shop for the growing list of items that I needed, as there was so much on my mind. It was all too overwhelming. I was starting Elijah and Sedaya's wardrobes from scratch and needed to buy everything: underwear, socks, shirts, shorts, pants, bathing suits, dresses, jackets, and hats.

I was standing in my favorite children's clothing store when the tears threatened to come once again. A friendly clerk came over and asked if there was anything she could help with. I told her briefly what was happening and what I needed. She had a quick look at my list, which also had the kids' most recent weights and measurements scribbled on it, and disappeared into the back room. She came out with armfuls of clothes that were extremely marked down and in the sizes that I needed. She even made some of the decisions for me. Once I had bought a few basics, I began to be able to think straight and join in on the shopping. The salesclerk's kindness and willingness to help did wonders to put me back into a functional mode. I was able to buy most of the clothing items and several sizes of shoes.

While in the mall, I felt hunger and thought about how long it had been since I had eaten—about a day and a half. I knew that to keep going, I would need to eat something. I stopped at a Dim Sum restaurant, which seemed like a good idea at the time. I had eaten Dim Sum only one other time, when Mark and I had gone on a weekend getaway to San Francisco. I reasoned that since the food is brought to your table, it would take less time. What I didn't factor in was my inability to make rational decisions, as my brain was on overload. I said yes to random food presented to me and then was unable to eat many of the dishes, as I am mostly vegetarian and I had accepted pork and beef items! I left the restaurant nearly as hungry as I had gone in and felt guilty about the food and money I had just wasted. I did some mental math and calculated how much food the money I had wasted could have bought my kids over in Ethiopia. I felt as low as if I had taken the food right out of their mouths.

Before going into the restaurant, I had called home for my messages. In addition to two requests from the media, which I ignored for the time being, there was a message from someone at the offices of BDO Dunwoody Limited, the appointed trustee handling the bankruptcy of Imagine Adoptions. I scribbled down the name and number and returned the call once seated in the eatery. The lady I first spoke to there was initially not very sympathetic to my plight. However, when she realized that I was one of the people whose children were in the Transition

Home and not one whose file was awaiting a referral, her tone changed and she quickly transferred me to someone higher up.

I felt badly for BDO, as they were used to handling bankruptcies that involved furniture or other possessions, not human lives. They'd had no idea when they initially got the files for Imagine Adoptions/KidsLink International that there were starving children in a foster home setting in Africa, and that the needs of these children would have to be addressed. They were now dealing with not only the urgent matter of what to do about those children's care, but also fielding calls from hundreds of people whose dreams of family were seemingly lost and whose emotions were understandably high.

I gave the woman the information I had about where we were at in terms of getting our kids home and asked her if there was anything she could do about our missing documents. She assured me that their top priority was working on a plan to ensure that the children were cared for until they could be united with their Canadian families. This was good to hear. It was a relief that they were working under the assumption of wanting to unite families, but she had no idea how to go about locating our documents and couldn't even suggest who we might be able to contact for help.

After the unsuccessful lunch attempt, I set off to a discount department store to begin shopping for toiletries and medications for Mark, as well as some things to amuse Elijah and Sedaya during the thirty-six hours of travel on the way home. While I was in the toy aisle, Mark phoned to let me know that he had managed to book a flight for himself leaving the coming Monday.

We also discussed what we would do about me traveling to meet him later. We decided that when we got word that the visas were going to be issued, I would book a flight to meet him and the kids in Ethiopia, and help bring them home. We knew that three flights over two or three days with two children who don't speak our language, and who were scared and fragile, would be next to impossible for him to handle alone.

That decision relieved some of our stress, but it also added a new problem. We needed to find someone to care for our other five children while we were gone. In our pre-bankruptcy plans, Mark's sister Aneta was going to come in November and stay in our home with our five kids. Other family members were going to help by taking them to their activities. In the current situation, however, Aneta was volunteering at a camp on a remote island and wasn't reachable. We needed a Plan B.

Mark began calling people we knew, starting with family and close friends, asking if they would be willing to take one of the kids. Our strategy was to split them all up and just ask people to take shifts of a few days each. I would likely be gone for close to two weeks, so we felt that people would be more likely to say yes if it was for a shorter commitment. The biggest problem we encountered was the time of year. Many of our friends and family members were going on summer vacation. As well, we were only able to give them an approximate timeline, since we had no firm plans until we knew more about when we could expect the visas.

Holly, who I had been friends with since the fourth grade, and who I would trust with any of my kids, was scheduled to leave on holidays around the time we estimated I would be gone. My friend Glenda, who would have been our first choice to take care of Josiah, was visiting her family in Trinidad. My mom had a full-time job. Most of Mark's family was going to be on holidays.

Many of our initial calls were unsuccessful. It was discouraging. Finding homes for all five of them for all the days I would be gone seemed like another insurmountable mountain. It looked like I may not be going to Ethiopia, after all.

While I was in the pharmacy section of the store, my cousin Don called me with an update. Don's good friend, Rob Merrifield, a member of the House of Commons in Canada and the Minister of State for Transport, had personally walked our email down to Minister Jason Kenney's office and hand-delivered it to him. Mr. Kenney was Canada's Minister of Immigration, and he now knew who our children were by name. He gave his commitment that when our documents were found, our visas would be processed immediately. Rob Merrifield asked Don to pass along to us that he and his wife would be praying for us and for our children. The blessings were flowing and I was struck by how much progress had already been made in just a few days.

Moments after speaking with Don, as I was searching for antifungal and antibiotic cream, my cell phone rang again. What I heard on that call humbled me to tears. On the other end of the phone were our friends Bonnie and Troy Sirette. They let me know that Mark had called them to ask if they would take one of our kids for a few days while I was in Ethiopia. They joked that they weren't willing to take one for a few days but they would take three or four for the entire time I was gone!

Their benevolence rendered me speechless. Bonnie and Troy had adopted their two girls from Ghana a year earlier and understood the unknowns we were facing. They also spoke to me about how excited they were for us and for the trip of a lifetime we were about to take. Their enthusiasm was such a departure from the bleakness we were encountering with others. Up to that point, I had been so focused on all the stress surrounding the trip that I hadn't allowed myself to see the positives or to feel any excitement about meeting our kids. Bonnie and Troy's joy was contagious, and as I paid for my cart full of purchases, I was smiling. I was beginning to believe that there might be a happy ending to this saga, after all.

One of our worries was financial. Though we were willing to do whatever it took to keep the kids safe, the thought of going deeply into debt for this trip added to our stress. Summer was high season and flights were going to cost us thousands more than they would have in the fall. Instead of buying the items we needed a little at a time, we had to buy them all at once. This was a concern.

An even larger financial concern was the income we were sure to lose with Mark being gone an indefinite amount of time. One of the ladies at his office generously offered to take over his files while he was gone, but there would still be a drastic drop in his earnings. When we'd held our garage sale fundraiser just a few months earlier, our motto had been "getting to Ethiopia ten cents at a time," so when I found a dime on the pavement that Wednesday, I knew it was no coincidence. I was reminded that God would provide the money somehow.

I picked up the kids at day camp, then retrieved Mackenzie from Diane's. Jonah had decided to stay another night and day, but Mackenzie was feeling a bit helpless about the situation and wanted to be back at home. Upon arriving home, the first thing I did was send another email to Mary at the Transition Home, asking her if she would kindly double-check the tracking number and get back to me when possible.

When checking my email, I was surprised to find half a dozen emails from reporters wanting to interview us. I was puzzled at how easily they had found ways to contact us. I would be even more shocked the next day when my cell phone began to ring constantly with requests from all forms of media. I still haven't figured out how my unlisted cell phone number got out.

Another email awaiting me was from the Alberta government, passing along the message that they had been asked by the officials in Nairobi to advise families not to travel to Africa until files could be reviewed. Families would be contacted once a decision was made. Reading this didn't make me doubt our decision for Mark to travel before we obtained the visas. I felt that most parents in our position would want to ensure the safety of their children, no matter what the officials were advising.

I took the time that night to check the adoption message boards again and was touched by a fund that had been started by other adoptive parents, some of whom were not affiliated with

70

Imagine Adoptions, to send money to the Transition Home to care for all the children there. Strangers from across the country were coming together, connected by a mutual goal. Ultimately, this group would raise over three thousand dollars that would later go towards donations at an orphanage in Ethiopia. People were already gathering money to ensure that the kids in the Transition Home were fed.

Another group that had also begun to form. When Imagine Adoptions was shut down, there were about four hundred families in the process of adopting, primarily from Ethiopia but also from Ghana, Ecuador, Brazil, and other countries. For the families not yet matched with children, the end of the agency also felt like the end of their long-held dream of family. It was shocking. It was devastating. But it united people from all across Canada who had a common hope. Out of the ashes of Imagine, a new group rose up. They were calling themselves FIA (Families of Imagine Adoptions) and the perseverance and conviction that these families showed under pressure was astounding! I was cheering their efforts in the background, but at the forefront of my mind was finding a way to get my kids home.

It was difficult to find any helpful information, as the tone on the message boards had shifted. Based on sheer numbers, the focus was on those who did not yet have referrals. There were so many threads pertaining to their efforts to revive the agency and to be able to complete their adoptions that the voices of those of us whose kids were in the Transition Home were drowned out. It became frustrating and time-consuming to find any information that applied to us.

Thankfully, I was able to ascertain a critical piece of information. Parents who had already arrived in Ethiopia since the bankruptcy had been allowed to take custody of their children. The reason this was an area of concern to me was that prior to this, parents had not been allowed to even meet their children at the Transition Home unless a visa had been issued by the Canadian government. We had even signed a document

71

at one time stating that we would not attempt to contact our children until we had our visa in hand. When the agency bankruptcy came to light and we decided that Mark would go to Ethiopia to protect our kids there, one question we had was whether or not he would be able to get custody of them once in Addis Ababa. Hearing that others who had already travelled to Ethiopia were meeting their children and were able to take them out of the home became one less stress for us to contend with.

I continued reading the message boards, where much of the talk was about what had triggered the freezing of the company's accounts and the sudden layoff of their staff. One thing that was clear by this point was that the bankruptcy was not due to lack of funds. Words swirling around, both online and in the media, were "misappropriation of funds," "mismanagement," "embezzlement," and "fraud." When I heard that some of the money had allegedly gone to pay for home renovations, a horse, and luxury trips, I felt physically ill. Elijah and Sedaya, who had already gone through so much in their tender years, now had to endure hunger in a home that we had trusted for their care while the Canadian woman at the head of the organization had been charging spa visits to the company and allegedly funneling money to an off-shore account. I had to turn away from the computer. It was too painful to continue reading the reports.

Wednesday, July 15, ended without any public statement issued by Imagine Adoptions, nor was there any comment made by Sue Hayhow, the agency's executive director. Imagine's website now only provided a link to the website of BDO Dunwoody, the bankruptcy trustees, where a general statement about the financials was given. No acknowledgement was made of the children stranded in the Transition Home. There were no instructions given as to how we should proceed or who we should go to for help.

I felt like I had accomplished a lot that day, but I also knew there was still much to do. While packing my new purchases, I was able to cross many items off the lists, but I had to add a few as well. That night, Mark stayed at the office most of the night trying to wrap up his professional commitments. Neither of us got much sleep, as we were overtired and wired on adrenaline. I was up often, checking the computer for word from Mary. As our night was daytime in Ethiopia, I knew that if I were to hear back, it would be during the night or early morning.

No word came that night.

CHAPTER ten

THURSDAY, JULY 16, BEGAN WITH A MORE SUBDUED TONE THAN THE OTHER days. I started the day off with my usual calls to Shelley and Lottie, but there was nothing new to report. My documents were still MIA and I was helpless to find them.

That morning, Mark and I began to discuss allowing the media to share our story. The agency's bankruptcy had already been top news across the country for the past few days, but much of the story was focused on the four hundred parents who were still awaiting a referral. These were the hundreds of people who might never have the chance to bring home their long-awaited children. With only forty-three children in the Transition Home, less than forty families were affected in the way we were, so there was a lot of media interest in sharing a story like ours.

We were very hesitant to go public, as we didn't welcome the scrutiny. However, as we felt that we had exhausted our other options and connections in trying to get our kids home, we decided to consent. We felt that the time had come to do this in the hopes that the story would encourage the government to further their efforts to speed up the processing of visas for all families involved. I also hoped that the continued involvement of the media would encourage the government to consider allowing the agency to continue in some capacity, which could

74

result in hundreds more Ethiopian children finding homes in Canada.

Mark and I decided that the only on-camera interview I would do would be with CBC Edmonton, as that was the station that the adoptive dad we knew worked for, and he assured us that it would be handled professionally. We knew that he understood adoption and we trusted him, even though he would not be the one conducting the interview. We also liked the fact that CBC would just be aired locally. I agreed to do two radio interviews as well.

We knew that agreeing to go public also meant that we would have to tell my parents, who were still enjoying their vacation and unaware of what was happening. I didn't want the first they heard of it to be on the news or through phone calls from their friends or family who had seen me on TV. I was glad that by the time I did call my mom, we had made some progress towards getting the Canadian government involved in speeding things up and we knew that Elijah and Sedaya had enough food to last until Mark arrived the following week.

I was still worried that calling my mom would ruin their trip, but I knew that it would be better if she heard it from me. There were some tears on both sides of the phone. By the end of our conversation, my mom had decided to come home a few days early, about which I felt both guilty and relieved. Knowing that my mom knew was another burden lifted, and after the news segment aired, she and my dad did get several calls on their cell phones, so I knew it had been the right decision to tell her when I did.

As I ran my errands that day, having Mackenzie with me was a nice distraction. He chatted aimlessly about things other than the adoption, things of interest to a teenage boy, but he also showed care and concern for me and for his new brother and sister. He gently reminded me that I should eat lunch. When I got busy running other errands and forgot, he took charge and told me that we needed to stop somewhere to eat. Realizing that my son needed to eat made it easier to take that time out and nourish myself as well. Whenever I would start to panic about details that needed to be worked out, Mackenzie would remind me to calm down and just take it one step at a time. It was a blessing to have that day with him.

Between dropping the younger kids off and picking them up, I had so much to do that it wasn't easy to fit in the TV interview. The reporter agreed to meet me at a nearby mall while I continued shopping for more items needed for packing. Obviously, my physical appearance was at the bottom of my priority list that week. When I left the house that morning, it was without knowing that I was going to be on camera that afternoon. There was little that I could do about my hair not being done, but as buying foundation was on my list anyway, I asked the lady at the makeup store if she could do a quick makeup application. Luckily, she was able to do it right away. I then met with the reporter and cameraman in the center of the mall.

The interview went well and Mackenzie was excited about making his TV debut, as he had been filmed walking beside me. I didn't give much thought to the piece after it was filmed, because I had so many other things to get done. I continued my shopping until it was time to pick the younger kids up and then went with them to the pharmacy to drop off Mark's and my prescriptions for antibiotics. I stopped at a sandwich shop on the way home to feed the kids and reminded myself to be sure to eat something once the kids were asleep.

Our friends Bonnie and Troy came over to give us travel tips and share information and stories with us about the year they'd spent in Ghana. They had also brought some items that would be useful for Mark on his trip. The visit with them was the first time that Mark and I had really sat down since the whole mess began. It was nice to be with people who were so positive and who had survived being in a foreign country waiting for visas with no clear deadline. Their positive outlook and open personalities energized us both.

After they left, we tried to watch my TV interview but realized that we didn't get the right channel. However, we heard late that night that a small segment of the interview had been aired on The National. We were able to catch the few minutes of my interview on The National, but we wondered how I'd ended up there. We were naïve about the press and didn't realize that one interview can later be rebroadcast on other stations. Apparently, my little interview was aired all across the country that night and the next day.

That night, I continued to check my emails whenever I couldn't sleep. Just before 3:00 a.m., I received a response from Mary at the Transition Home. She had included another tracking number that she was sure was the right one. I hesitantly went over to the DHL website and typed in the digits. I was able to see that the package had, indeed, made it to the Canadian High Commission and been signed for on July 8. I took down the name of the person who had signed for it and looked forward to being able to pass it on to Lottie when the MP's office opened for the day. Being able to prove that our documents were in Nairobi and were the responsibility of that office was a huge step towards securing visas for the kids.

I was starting to sense a change in the way things were heading and we were no longer feeling that Mark would have to spend months away. There were even wonderful moments of excitement amongst the stressful ones. I cherished those.

There had been a point some years back when Mark and I had considered having another biological child. I had heard of a medication that would probably be able to alleviate the symptoms of the condition I had experienced during my pregnancies. Because of this, we had looked into the possibility of another pregnancy, even going so far as to schedule an appointment for Mark to have his vasectomy reversed. The closer that date came, though, the more we got to thinking about what it would mean to have another biological child. We finally came to the conclusion that it was not the right decision for us. For us to have another biological child would mean us adopting one less child, and we had come to be aware of how many children out there needed loving homes. It seemed that once we knew that, choosing pregnancy simply because it was less complicated or more convenient would have been wrong for us; it would have meant us turning our backs on those children. We had already experienced the amazing journey of adoption and didn't want to rob ourselves of the chance to see what other children God had in store for our family.

I didn't have to wonder if I could love an adopted child as much as I loved my biological children. The question that so many people who are considering adoption ask themselves and don't dare speak out loud had already been answered for me in the form of three precious blessings. I cannot say if it would be the same for everyone, but I already had the answer to that question: for me, it was a resounding yes! I could say with absolute certainty that I loved my adopted children as much as the ones I had carried within me for nine months and with whom I shared a biological connection.

In fact, there was an added component to my love for the adopted children, a fierceness that was almost primal. My adopted children had been hurt. Whether through prenatal exposure, neglect, or abuse, they had all suffered. Knowing of their pain at such young ages brought out the mother bear in me, the instinct to protect them from further harm. I wanted to allow them to feel a love so strong that it could, perhaps, partly make up for any feelings of abandonment and rejection they might someday face. I wanted to give them every opportunity to reach their fullest potential.

Mark and I are not perfect parents, but we have always tried to create an environment for our kids that will allow them to reach their greatest potential as individuals. We want to raise them in a setting where they can be themselves and know beyond a doubt that they are loved and worth loving. Although we do feel that we are helping by adopting children who are in need of a family, I know that the blessings we have received from parenting these children far outweigh any ways in which we have enriched their lives. Parenting each one of our children, those gifted to us by birth and those gifted to us through adoption, has been the greatest privilege of my life.

eleven

THERE WAS AN AIR OF EXPECTANCY ON THE MORNING OF JULY 17. ARMED WITH proof of our documents' arrival at their intended destination, I felt a shift. That day, a friend of ours organized a day of prayer and fasting for us and our kids. It was as though I could feel the prayers lifting me up and carrying me through. I should have had no energy with the lack of sleep and food, but I felt as if I could conquer the world.

I was able to read some of the prayers that had been sent for the special day of prayer and fasting:

> *God, in your mercy, make a way where there seems no way. Give divine wisdom and appointments for the people they need to contact, and bring the children in safety and peace into their new lives. Father, send forth ministering angels from Your very presence to surround those children. Send ravens to feed them and a loving hand to comfort and tenderly care for them. And for these new parents and family members, send amazing peace which passes all human understanding, that they may confidently trust in You, Your timing, and abundant provision.*

> *Take courage that the entire situation is in God's hands. He can do miracles. All things are possible to Him.*

Dear Father God, we ask You to protect and provide for these orphans and those who are attempting to rescue them. Lord, just as you fed five thousand from a small basket lunch, I pray You will provide and multiply all resources to save these children and those with hearts who desire their safety and protection. We know how you have a special place in your heart for children. Their angels are always before you. And Jesus said, "Let the little children come to me, and do not hinder them, for the kingdom of God belongs to such as these. I tell you the truth, anyone who will not receive the kingdom of God like a little child will never enter it. And he took the children in his arms, put his hands on them and blessed them" *(Mark 10:14–16). We praise you, Father, for your wondrous love and compassion.*

We pray that you would feel our Abba father's arms around you as He loves all *your children even* more *than you as a human could. Amazing love!*

Praying for a fishes-and-loaves provision and travel mercies for them all. Praying for resurrection and flourishing of the adoption agency. God bless all those who go through the work to adopt the less fortunate.

I just lift up these little angels in the orphanage in Ethiopia. God, I pray for your hand of protection upon them. Lord, you have already handpicked and set aside two little ones for this family and I pray that before anything serious happens to them because of this money situation that you will move them from Ethiopia into their intended home. Lord, your will is not to let these little ones suffer, and I pray that you intervene in a way that only you can. Your word says to let the little ones come to you, and that's what we are praying, Lord. Draw them near to you and keep them safe.

Father, provide miraculously for all the needs that Elijah and Sedaya have. Give peace to Sharla, Mark, and the kids, and wisdom to know the next step. We claim these children for this family in Jesus' name.

Reading some of the prayers being spoken for us and our children from people who knew us, and from people who didn't, was just the push I needed to keep going. I knew that this was all in God's hands.

When I began to run my errands that day, there was a change in how I viewed what I was doing. When I went to the bank to get American money for Mark to take on the trip, I was excited by the prospect of him using the money to pay a driver to take him from the airport to where our children were, or paying for food to feed the mouths that a week earlier I had not been able to guarantee would get fed.

When I went to the bookstore to buy a picture dictionary, it was with dreams of the first communications I would encounter with Elijah and Sedaya. When I went to pick up the antibiotics from the pharmacy for Mark and myself, it was with the realization that we were really both going to be able to be with our new children in their home country and bring them back to Canada together.

I came home in between some of my errands and was surprised to see a message on the computer from my caseworker at Imagine. Her words were just further evidence of the goodness that exists. I knew that there were people everywhere praying on our behalf.

I just wanted to let you know that I am devastated by what has happened. I am so thankful your court went through the first time. Although I am no longer employed by Imagine, I would very much like to hear when your children have arrived safely home. I am praying for all the families and children and trust God has an amazing plan. My work with Imagine was more than a job, as I came to care for each family I worked with and the precious children they were matched with. I fully understand if you wish to not respond, but I will continue to pray for you.

I had never harbored any hard feelings towards the staff at the agency after the scandal broke out. Sue Hayhow, Rick Hayhow, and Andrew Morrow were the ones being criminally investigated, and it was obvious to me that most of the other staff would not have been involved in anything untoward.

In fact, that week, some of the agency's former staff came forward and volunteered their time to help BDO Dunwoody in any way they could. There were women working from their kitchen tables with their personal computers, doing what they could to help the affected families. These were women who had just found themselves out of a paying job and had their own stresses to contend with, but they selflessly gave of their own time and resources to help in whatever capacity they could.

After a brief stop at home, I went to a coffee shop to meet Shelley and a reporter from our local newspaper. She and I both wanted to ensure that Leon Benoit received positive press about his efforts to help us. There were many MPs in other parts of Canada who had refused to get involved to help families in their riding who were in the same position as us, and we were grateful to Mr. Benoit and Lottie for their help. Lottie had been phenomenal and she remained my first business call every morning. That day, she was working behind the scenes to encourage Nairobi to find our documents now that she had the date that the documents had been signed for in their office.

Our interview with the local reporter didn't take long. The mood was lighter than it had been all week, especially because Shelley and her husband had gotten word that the visa for their son might be finished and they were making travel plans. My thoughts were now about *when* we brought Elijah and Sedaya home, not *if* we were able to bring them home.

Once I had picked up the kids, I stopped by my mom's empty house to pick up a flashlight she had said I could borrow to send with Mark, as there are frequent power outages in Addis Ababa. While at my mom's, a reporter from the Edmonton Journal called my cell and asked to interview me for an article they wanted to run. I agreed to the interview, but only over the phone, as I was too busy to arrange it any other way.

I became increasingly apprehensive during our brief conversation, because she seemed to want to focus on the fact that Mark was traveling to Ethiopia before we had visas for the kids, which was against the wishes of the Alberta government. Certainly we had received one email that advised us not to travel before we had been given word that the visas were ready, but we had spoken to staff in the government office in question that were sympathetic to our situation and supportive of our decision to travel right away. It was not as though we were trying to be rebellious or that we were breaking any laws. We were doing everything in our power to ensure the safety of our children.

The way she worded her questions implied that we were defying authority. This had me concerned enough to decide during that call that other than an upcoming radio interview to which I had already committed, this would be my last media interview on the subject. Mark was increasingly uneasy about the snowball effect of the tiny amount of press I had done. I was now receiving requests from across Canada and the United States for interviews by television stations, newspapers, and radio. I was out of my element. Even though it had just begun a day before, it already felt like it had gotten out of control.

I stopped at the mailbox, which was by now stuffed full of bills and fliers. In going through the mail, I came across two envelopes that weren't bills. One contained a check for one hundred dollars towards our adoption and a note explaining that it was God's money and would be used for His will. The other was a thank-you card sent from friends in B.C. who had stayed with us overnight a few weeks before. The envelope was post-marked for the previous Saturday, so it had been sent before news came out about the bankruptcy. Within the card was a check for two hundred dollars to be put towards our Ethiopia travel fund. It amazed me how at a time where I barely had the words or time to utter prayers, God was still answering them.

Seeing that this money had been sent before the story came out was further proof that God had known the timing all along and would continue to meet our needs.

Mark came home late again that day, as it was his last business day before he trip. There was more to do than there were hours left. After the kids were in bed, I went online again and was dismayed to read the atrocious comments that had been made in response to the media report I had done. Some of the comments were so ignorant that they didn't bother me, such as that we were just using children as fashion accessories or trying to be trendy and follow Angelina Jolie.

I knew that Mark and I had started our road in adoption long before it became fashionable. I also found it disgusting that people would see an increase in the popularity of adoption as a celebrity trend, instead of an indication of a positive social change. As a matter of fact, adoptions were decreasing in number, not increasing as the public perception falsely stated.

One comment, laughable in its lack of thought, blasted us for contributing to the demise of the world by having a large family and therefore increasing our carbon footprints. The ignorance of that comment was that all the children we had adopted already existed in the world; their "carbon footprint" was unchanged. All we were doing was giving them a family. By far the most common negative comment had to do with our adopting internationally when there were so many Canadian children who needed homes. This was hurtful to me, since I am an advocate of all adoption and I felt that we had already played a part within the Canadian adoption system by adopting three children, two of whom had special needs and were technically considered "hard to place."

By choosing to adopt internationally, we were choosing to help two more children who needed a family. It was as simple as that. It wasn't that we felt children in other parts of the world were more deserving of a family, only perhaps that there was more need present there. I was outraged that we were under attack for our choice to care for orphans and I posted a comment in reply. I declared that I was the person spoken of in the article, and that although I wouldn't dignify the comments about children as fashion accessories with a response, I wanted to point out that we had adopted three of our children from within the regional foster care system. I hoped that this information would put to rest any further judgments on that particular aspect of the story.

Reading all the negative backlash was exhausting. I would learn in the coming days that it was best not to search our names on the internet or to read or listen to the responses that were to come. I had started the day feeling encouraged and energized, but was now feeling spent and scrutinized. I questioned why God had sent us down this road and then put obstacles in our path.

Soon after, I received a compassionate email from a reporter who had read the comments on one of the online stories, as well as my response. He asked me to please phone him to confirm that it was me who had written the follow-up comment and to confirm that we had adopted from within Canada. He was very apologetic for the public opinion expressed so cruelly and wished to have my permission to add a line to the existing story to note that we had already adopted three children provincially. It was another kind gesture from a stranger. The kindness of friends and strangers was holding me up. Their prayers were carrying me when I felt that I could no longer carry myself.

Another bright spot this day was that a lady on one of the adoption message boards, Christy, had stepped forward with an idea to help those of us waiting for visas. She was not in this position herself, as she was already home with her adopted daughter, but she had noticed that in the frantic efforts by the hundreds of other families to restructure the adoption agency and revive their dreams of family, our small group had been largely lost in the mix and it was becoming difficult for us to receive and share information. She came up with an idea to contact each of us and to create a private group with a message board that only we could access. Rather than sorting through dozens, or even hundreds, of messages daily that didn't apply to us, the private message board would allow us to access the ones that would be helpful to us in our situation. It was so thoughtful of her to take the time to care for us and to spearhead this idea, especially since none of us involved had the time or the brain space to be able to make this a reality.

Christy was also very knowledgeable about the immigration process and lent us her expertise. The information was wonderful, but the support and encouragement from her and the others on the new message board was invaluable, because they were in the same position we were and truly understood. The group was aptly named "Operation Visa," and its birth meant that I no longer had to spend what had become very precious time checking the other message boards for any shred of new information. It also meant that we all had a safe place to share our fears, frustrations, and hopes. It was becoming evident that the Canadian High Commission was, indeed, processing visas for those children caught in the bankruptcy as quickly as it could. The best part of the new group was the spirit of celebration whenever it was announced that another visa had come through.

Late Friday night, when all the kids were sleeping and Mark had gotten home from work, he and I made ourselves a tray of nachos, tortilla chips heaping with gooey melted cheese, tomatoes, onions, and spicy, fresh jalapenos, which is my ultimate comfort food, and sat down together in front of the TV. It was the first time all week that we had relaxed, and we chose a mindless show that would require no thought from us whatsoever.

For the first time in five days, I allowed my mind to be somewhere other than on Elijah and Sedaya. It was bliss!

twelve

SATURDAY, JULY 17, WAS THE MOST EMOTIONALLY CHALLENGING DAY FOR ME
all week. During the weekdays, it felt like I was actively doing
something to get Elijah and Sedaya safely home, but with the
government offices closed both in Canada and in Africa over
the weekend, I couldn't advocate for them. There was no daily
phone check-in with Lottie or with anyone in Alberta Children's
Services. In addition, with less time spent on the phone, there
was also more time to think… and the thinking quickly turned
to worrying. I tried to turn every worried thought into prayer,
but doubts followed me like shadows, darkening every turn.

I was aware that it wasn't possible that I was surviving on my
own strength given the week I had endured. I felt like God was
holding me up, but I could also feel the fears pulling at me and
whispering their lies.

I had already agreed to do a radio interview, but I was
nervous going in, since the negative comments we had gotten
after my other press interviews were nagging at me. With his trip
approaching, Mark was nervous that all the attention would lead
to the media being present when his plane landed in Ethiopia.
He worried that this could cause problems for him with officials
there, especially with the shifted focus on him traveling there
supposedly against the wishes of our own government. Still

hearing Mark's words and the opinions of naysayers in my head, I fumbled my way through the radio interview, nervous of saying something that could be misconstrued or used out of context. I was sweating by the time the short talk was over. I felt dejected.

That day, we were blessed to receive a meal from another family. I revised my freezer meal plan and made a grocery list to prepare for it. There was still so much to be done. What we had planned to do over a three-and-a-half-month period now had to be done in one week. I was frazzled.

Mark and I finished packing for his trip. He was intent on only bringing one small suitcase with him, which I found ridiculous. It was nearly impossible to pack for him and two kids in one suitcase. He only brought a few outfits for each of them and for himself, reasoning that he could have laundry done there when they ran short of clothes. He consented to bringing some of the medication in case he or they needed it.

I had packed all kinds of activities for the kids to do, but he unpacked them all, not wanting them to take up room in his bag. I was finally able to convince him to let me repack a skipping rope and an inflatable beach ball, as well as water wings in case they went swimming. I packed the rest of the clothes and toys in suitcases to bring with me.

Diane Carpenter, who had helped so much already by taking Mackenzie and Jonah for most of the week, bringing meals, offering encouraging words, and helping at our previous fundraisers, came forward to help even more. She, along with other friends Cyndie Zinger and Lorraine Stephanyshyn, organized a bottle drive fundraiser and a silent auction, with all proceeds going towards the expenses that our family and Shelley's family were encountering. It was such a blessing to have a community of people supporting us and taking care of the details.

Our local paper ran a write-up about the fundraising efforts and people spread the word online. I was in awe of their generosity and practical expression of love for our family. In all, almost two thousand dollars was raised. We knew that once we got to Ethiopia, our expenses would be higher than we were originally expecting. This was because of the higher cost of summer flights and because the agency was obviously no longer providing services such as transportation, traditional Ethiopian outfits for the kids, and a cultural evening. We knew that we could skip the cultural evening, but transportation would be pretty essential!

We got in touch with the Ethiopian man we had sat with at the Hope International dinner half a year earlier. He spoke to Mark and later emailed him the phone numbers for his sister and nephew in Ethiopia. It was looking less likely that Mark would have to stay for months, but we wanted to be prepared for anything.

On Sunday, Shelley and her husband received confirmation from the embassy that their son's visa had been issued. I was overjoyed for them! A month or so earlier, Shelley had sent me an email on the day we had received copies of our kids' documents. In it, she had written that she was sure she and I would both be in Ethiopia at the same time. I had laughed at the comment, as she was to be traveling two to three months before we were. Now here we were, both preparing to travel at the same time and making plans to get together in another country!

Originally, Imagine had two Transition Homes in Addis Ababa, one where the older children were and another one for babies. In an effort to conserve the little money they had left, the caregivers there had moved the babies into the home with the older children. We knew that this meant another change for our kids, as the babies and their caregivers were now there and some of the caregivers had left. With frantic parents arriving almost daily at this point to pick up their children, and all the changes, it would have been impossible for our kids to be unaware that something was going on. I wished that there was some way of letting them know that they had not been forgotten, that they were loved beyond measure, and that their new daddy was on his way to get them.

Also on Sunday, we got word that a company had stepped in and donated $100,000 to fund the Transition Home and the care of the children there until all the kids could safely come home. Some of the kids had been matched with families in Canada, but hadn't yet had successful court dates, so it would be many months before they would be able to come home. News that the caregivers in Ethiopia would begin getting paid again and that there would be sufficient food and supplies for the children there, as well as access to medical care, was an enormous relief.

The company that donated this huge sum of money to ensure the continued care of the kids was Yamana Gold, Inc. a Canadian-based gold production company. We were touched that people who had no personal association with Imagine Adoptions would even consider having their company provide aid to children they had never met. What an unexpected blessing! This gift meant that all the families whose children were at the Transition Home were provided with peace of mind, especially those whose children would be there for an extended time.

It's hard to explain how much I was thinking about Elijah and Sedaya, and how much I missed them. Saying that I missed them might sound strange, because I had never met them. A week earlier, I hadn't been missing them. I had been excited to meet them and thought of them often, but it wasn't the constant, near obsessive preoccupation like I was presently experiencing. Now, I was always wondering, "Are they scared? Do they realize what is about to happen? Are they hungry? Is someone explaining things to them? Will we be allowed to bring them home?" I hadn't realized the depth of my love for them until the day of the bankruptcy.

There's an expression about parents going to the ends of the earth for their children. Well, now we were about to do just that!

Kostelyk family, 2008

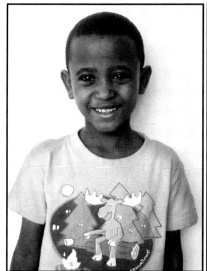
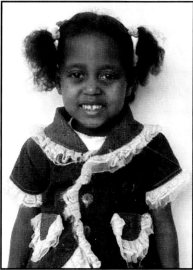

Seeing pictures of our son, Elijah and our daughter, Sedaya,
for the first time, May 22, 2009

Mark's first meeting with the kids, July 22, 2009

My first day with the kids, stopping for lunch at the African Safari Lodge after visiting Faya Orphanage

Beautiful Ethiopia

Elijah and Sedaya with Auntie Deanne on our last day in Ethiopia

Our family finally united! Edmonton International Airport August 6, 2009
(photo credit: Matt Aubin)

Mark and Mackenzie's trip to Ethiopia in November, 2010

Kostelyk family, 2011 (photo credit: Matt Aubin)

thirteen

ON MONDAY, JULY 20, THE KIDS AND I DROVE MARK TO THE AIRPORT TO SAY goodbye. It was heart-wrenching for me to imagine that I would not be there when he first met Elijah and Sedaya. I wouldn't be there to experience the first precious moments my husband would share with our son and daughter. It took a lot of internal dialogue not to book myself on the next flight out.

Immediately after leaving the airport, I received the news that our supporting documents were still missing somewhere in the office in Nairobi. When we had confirmed the tracking numbers and proven that the documents had arrived where they were supposed to, I had assumed that they would swiftly be found and all would then go smoothly. In order for our kids' visas to have made the time cutoff to be in the diplomatic pouch sent to Ethiopia that week, they would have to be issued by the next day. The news sunk my hopes of flying out later that week to join Mark and the kids. It was another low point for me.

Mark called me from the airport in Toronto. He was worried when I told him that my one little news clip from the other night's television interview had been on CNN that day. He was concerned that there would be reporters when he got to Ethiopia. All we could do was pray that there wouldn't. Thankfully, he arrived to no fanfare.

That afternoon, when I had to go to the lawyer's office to sign for our real estate sale, I had to bring all five kids with me. It was hectic, but the lawyer was kind enough to do things as quickly as he could and I was able to cross one more thing off my list of things to do. I also had to take the kids with me to renew our house insurance and run other errands that were equally boring for them. We still had so much left to do and I wasn't looking forward to taking five grouchy kids to Costco! The day seemed long and I felt very discouraged.

I turned on the radio and the heard the song "Mighty to Save." It was the first time since the crisis started that I cried happy tears, because I knew beyond a doubt in that moment that God would get our kids home. The lyrics playing at the time were:

Savior, He can move the mountains.
My God is mighty to save.
He is mighty to save.
Forever, author of salvation,
He rose and conquered the grave.
Jesus conquered the grave.[1]

I knew that a God who could move mountains and conquer the grave could get our kids visas, and He could surely bring them home. It might take a miracle, but I was choosing to believe in one.

That night, I spoke again to my sister-in-law Deanne. I called to update her on where we were at and to ask her to continue praying that our documents would be found. I was still so disappointed that she wasn't going to be able to make the trip to Ethiopia with us. However, I knew that I was nowhere near as disappointed as she was, so I was careful with my choice of words when I spoke about the upcoming trip.

[1]Story, Laura. "Mighty to Save." *Great God Saves.* INO Records, 2008.

Deanne had a surprise for me, though. She was able to get time off work and was going to be able to come with me to Ethiopia, after all! It was a giant relief, as I had never travelled outside of North America and I was nervous about traveling alone. It would be such a blessing to have her company. Also, because we weren't sure yet if Mark would be able to change his ticket and get on the same flight as us going home, I was faced with the prospect of flying by myself with two children who didn't speak the same language as me, who may have diarrhea from parasites, and who would be in the midst of the biggest transition and upheaval of their lives. The thought of undertaking three days and three separate flights with them by myself terrified me. Knowing I wouldn't be making the trip alone took away my worries and made me feel as if God had taken care of yet another detail. As Deanne and I spoke about the trip, excitement crept in and I even found myself laughing.

On Tuesday, July 20, God moved a mountain for us; our missing documents were found and I was told that we would be getting a decision on the status of our kids' visas by Friday! With that hope, I took a leap of faith and booked flights for Deanne and me, and booked Elijah and Sedaya on our return flights.

Deanne and I would be flying out of Edmonton on Monday, July 27. It took nine hours to get the flights booked. It wouldn't have been possible to do this while supervising the other kids, but another blessing arrived that day as well. Before Christmas, we were saddened when our amazing babysitter Mandi moved to another province. We hadn't found another babysitter. However, just a few weeks earlier, Mandi had moved back to town. When she heard what was happening, she offered to come and play with the kids. She refused to let me pay her and stayed all day.

Mandi was helpful, kind, and gifted with children. She was more than a babysitter to us; she had become a friend, and was such a blessing in our lives. Knowing that she was living nearby again eased some of the worry about how I would cope when I got home and had seven kids to care for, as I knew we could access her help from time to time. Her being there that day also helped to ease the guilt I had been feeling about dragging the kids around and not doing anything fun with them. I knew that they were having a great day with Mandi to entertain them and giving them her attention. I knew the kids needed my attention, too, but substituting hers was the best I could offer them at the time.

That morning, while waiting to hear back from a travel agent about our flights, I went shopping for the large list of groceries I needed for the freezer meal recipes. I went by myself to Save-On Foods, my usual grocery store. I had the list in hand, but found myself overwhelmed again, not knowing where to start.

I was approached by Petra, a store employee who had always been friendly when I went through her till. She had even let some of my kids do the scanning on occasion. She and I had chatted before and she knew about our adoption plans. She commented on me not having the kids with me and noted that I looked lost. I briefed her on what was happening. She took a look at my list and went to speak to the meat manager. She offered to get the meat together and have it rung in and waiting for me at the front to save time. I was very grateful and set about getting the other items.

When I'd found everything on the list, I went to the front and discovered that the store manager had donated some freezer bags for us to put the meat in, and had given me a discount on the meat. I was even more touched when Petra came running up to give me a bag with two items she had purchased herself; she had bought Elijah and Sedaya activity books for the plane ride home. She was excited for me and asked me to bring the kids in to the store to meet her once we were settled in back at home. I was once again moved by the support we were receiving in the most unexpected places.

In the late afternoon, my sister-in-law Stephanie came by and picked up a bunch of the vegetables I had bought. She also took some chicken to cut up so that it would be easier to assemble the freezer meals. She did all the chopping even though it was her anniversary, a day which she could have spent pampering herself. *It takes a village*, I reminded myself. There were so many people helping in whatever way they could to prepare for Elijah and Sedaya's arrival.

I stayed up late once again, copying out recipes for the freezer meals and setting out stations to assemble each one. I labeled dozens of bags with the cooking instructions. I fried up the veggie beef and made a few of the meals. After the kids were asleep, it was eerily quiet in the house and I used the time to pray for Mark on his travels, and for Elijah and Sedaya. I also prayed for our other kids and the huge adjustment they would have in the coming weeks and months. I felt peaceful one second and nervous the next, imagining how Mark's first meeting with the kids would go.

Mark emailed me from the airport in Dubai, giving me detailed instructions for navigating the Toronto and Dubai airports. I was grateful for any tips he had, since neither Deanne nor I had travelled much. We were unsure of certain things, such as whether to pick up our bags in Dubai or to simply pack things in our carry-ons for the overnight stay there. Deanne and I were also a bit nervous about the size of the airports we would be going to.

Mark was about five hours away from arriving in Ethiopia and would be meeting our kids shortly after that. I was excited for him, but at the same time I felt sad.

fourteen

WEDNESDAY, JULY 22, WAS A MILESTONE DAY. IT WAS EXACTLY TWO MONTHS from the day we had signed our acceptance papers for Elijah and Sedaya and one month to the day that a court had declared them our children.

It was also the day Mark met them for the first time.

Our care packages had arrived at the Transition Home just days earlier and our kids had been shown our pictures and told that their daddy was going to be coming to pick them up in a few days. Elijah would later tell us that he thought we looked nice and that he liked getting the same shirt as the one his new brothers and dad were wearing in the pictures. He would also later tell us that he was scared of Mark those first days and that no one had explained to him that he would be coming with us to Canada.

When Mark arrived, the kids were wearing the clothes we had sent in the Ziplocs. He spent two hours with them in the courtyard, letting them get used to him and playing with them. Elijah played catch with Mark, but was quite reserved. Sedaya was goofy and a bit of a ham. She made faces at him, trying to get him to laugh. Elijah and Sedaya fought, as siblings tend to do, over Mark's digital camera.

When Mark called me in the middle of the night (daytime where he was), he said to me, "You know when we used to get foster kids, and sometimes we would get an older one where right away we would be able to see ourselves adopting them? Well, they are a thousand times cuter than that and I totally have that same feeling, but way more."

He was smitten! It was great to hear his reaction, but it stung not to have been there to share those first moments. I also wished that I would have been able to meet the caregivers personally and thank them for caring for our kids and not abandoning them even when their pay had stopped.

My day that Wednesday was very different than Mark's. At sunrise, I was outside in our backyard. One moment I was looking out at our property, marveling at the beautiful land that God had blessed us with, and in the next moment I was sobbing about the possibility of never seeing Elijah and Sedaya play on the swing set or running on the lawn with our other kids. Right there, I chose to claim the promise that He had put these kids in our hearts long ago and I would see them laugh and play here one day.

My mom and Diane took the kids to their houses for the day. My friends Grayce and Kathy came over to help me assemble the freezer meals. Both women worked hard and were positive and encouraging. I listened to the Amharic CD in the background. It was another exhausting but productive day.

By day's end, the house smelled of garlic and onions and we had finished making more than sixty meals. I also managed to book Mark on our flight home, which was comforting. Providing that the visas came in time, Mark, Deanne, and I would all be flying home together with Elijah and Sedaya. I tried to keep my excitement tempered, but it was there, building as the hours counted down.

Thursday, July 23, was devoted to ensuring that our other kids would be taken care of while I was away. I began to pack for them and I made a box of gifts for them to get each day while we were gone, to help them count down the time. I found two families willing to take care of Jonah while we were away, the

Zingers and the Buchholtzs. My niece Katie and her husband agreed to take Mackenzie for most of the time I would be gone, with the help of some other family members. There were three dates at the end of my trip when people would be away on holidays and I couldn't find anyone to care for Mackenzie, Josiah, Gracelyn, or Eliana. Eventually it was decided that if we couldn't find anyone else, my mom would take the days off work to care for them.

I made lists for each of the kids, providing important information such as phone numbers and allergy and medical information. I contacted Gracelyn's pulmonary specialist, to apprise him of the situation, and passed his phone numbers along to Bonnie and Troy. As well, I gave them detailed instructions for her medical care. I renewed all of her prescriptions, just in case any of them were to run out while I was gone.

Over in Ethiopia, Mark was in the lobby of the guest house where he was staying when he ran into Ted Giesbrecht. Ted was a lawyer whose services had been acquired by BDO Dunwoody to travel to Ethiopia and oversee the handling of the necessary paperwork to complete the adoptions and secure visas for all forty-three children in the Transition Home so that they could come to Canada. Ted was very experienced in adoption and he was volunteering his skills to facilitate the best possible outcomes in the shortest amount of time.

In addition to securing paperwork, Ted arranged for medicals to be done on those who needed them for permanent resident visas, and he also brought children to have their pictures taken for their new passports. He was in contact with the embassy and with the caregivers at the Transition Home. Ted had a list of all the families he had been told were in Ethiopia waiting for visas, but our names had been overlooked. When Mark just happened to run into Ted there, he made Ted aware of our specific situation and Mark was able to sign papers granting Ted permission to act on our behalf.

As Ted had the power to speak directly to the Canadian High Commission regarding our file, this chance meeting proved invaluable. Ted would be informed directly if there was anything missing from our files or if any additional information was needed. He would be told when a decision was made in our case.

Mark spent time with Elijah and Sedaya again, but the time difference and the frequent power outages there made it difficult for Mark and me to communicate. Sometime after 2:00 a.m., after a marathon of laundry and packing, I fell asleep only to be woken by the phone shortly after 3:00. Mark was calling with an emergency. Ted had received information about our file and passed the concern along to Mark. That impromptu meeting in the lobby of the guest house was already helping us. Imagine Adoptions hadn't included our provincial letter of no objection with the documents they sent, and the visas couldn't be issued without it. Since we had originally forwarded the copy our province had sent us, we didn't have a backup copy to send. I needed to get another one issued from the Alberta government.

I immediately sent an email to the woman I had been in contact with at Alberta Children's Services. It was early Friday morning. By the time she got to her office, Nairobi would be closed for the weekend, so our visas would not be issued that day. I would be traveling to Ethiopia not knowing if we were going to be able to get visas for the kids or not. I was able to reach her by phone that morning. She was aware of the situation and had forwarded the letter of no objection to the High Commission.

I then phoned Lottie at the MP's office to give her an update of the new development and she told me that she had heard that the rest of our files were complete and that the visas would be issued once this was resolved. That was reassuring, but the uncertainty of traveling to Africa without a guarantee of being able to bring home our children was unnerving.

I heard from Mark later that morning as he was heading over to the Transition Home to take permanent custody of our kids.

He laughed when he let me know that he was already regretting unpacking the games, books, and play dough I had originally put in his suitcase. He was very thankful for the jump rope and was hoping the beach ball wouldn't spring a leak!

He had bought a cord for the camera and emailed me some pictures of his first two meetings with the kids. It was joyous to see their smiles. Seeing them with Mark healed many of my worries, but it stung not to be there. I had never imagined that our first pictures of meeting the kids in Ethiopia wouldn't include me. Mark was worried about the language barrier and being on his own with them for a full week. However, he was relieved to hear that Deanne would be traveling with me, so he would have one less thing to worry about.

Seeing the pictures and knowing everything it had taken just to get to that point made other considerations seem silly. During preparation for our planned November trip, we had decided that we were going to buy a video camera to record the first moments of meeting the kids. We were also going to buy a digital still camera so that we would have better quality pictures for me to scrapbook later. I had even planned out which pictures to take and what I would be wearing! Now, we had no video of this first meeting and no fancy camera to capture the moment, but looking at the grainy photos Mark had sent me, I cared only that the kids were safe and with him. Our kids at home began to call Mark "the hero daddy," because he had gone to Ethiopia to rescue their brother and sister. When I saw those pictures, all I saw were my two children, alive and smiling, sitting with their hero daddy.

It was another day of blessings for us, a day of feeling thankful that so many wonderful people were supporting us, that Mark was in Ethiopia with our kids, and that it looked likely that we were all going to be together soon. On realizing that Mark had our kids with him, my thoughts turned to those families on the road to adoption who did not yet have their referrals, who had been waiting weeks, months, and even years, those whose dreams of growing their family were now uncertain. They were grieving an incredible loss and I was aware that we were actually the lucky ones.

There had been days the week before when it didn't feel that way, when it felt like the floor had been moved out from under me, when we heard that the children we had loved from afar might starve. There had been days of rumors of the adoption being overturned, when it looked as if our family would be separated for months. There were days of worry, days of panic, days of pain, but this day, with an end in sight, staring at a photograph of my husband holding our two Ethiopian children, I knew that we would be bringing our children home. We were the ones who would have the privilege of raising them.

I looked ahead to the day when all my children would be here, together, and couldn't help but smile. We were blessed. That night, I wrote these words:

Adoption truly does change lives. It changes life forever for a child who needs a home, whether it be a child in Canada or a child in an impoverished country. It changes life for a family that gets to experience the joy of raising that child. Such people are often able to appreciate being parents that much more because the road to get there isn't an easy one.

I hope that what has transpired in the past week and a half doesn't deter anyone from adopting. I hope that perhaps it will even serve to inspire. In our case, through the evidence of miracles, because when our children come home, it will be nothing short of one.

Hope exists even in the case of those still waiting for referrals. Their determination to see their dreams of a family realized shows the depths of love they have for their future children. I hope that one day, each one of them will come to know firsthand the beauty, joy, and love that adoption can bring as they welcome their new children.

fifteen

SATURDAY, JULY 25, WAS A BLUR OF FINISHING EVERYTHING I COULD AROUND the house. I made another dozen freezer meals and double-checked what I had packed for the kids and for myself. I filled two backpacks with little toys and activities for Elijah and Sedaya for their flights home.

In the afternoon, Diane Carpenter came and stayed with the kids while I finished up some shopping. I took Jonah with me and it was nice to spend some one-on-one time with him. I knew that in the weeks after we got home with the new kids, one-on-one time with any of the kids would be scarce. I also took the time later that evening to read to the three younger kids. At bedtime, I took extra moments with their tuck-ins, sneaking in some long cuddles knowing that it would be two weeks before I'd get to kiss them goodnight again.

That night, my friend Holly came over and helped me with some of the last-minute preparations. Holly and I even had fun using a home kit to cover the grey in my hair. She laughed at how complicated the Amharic on my CD sounded, but she was impressed with the progress I had made so far in mastering a few phrases. Although it felt like the list of things to do was endless, I was thankful for all the help I had received over the past two weeks.

Sunday, July 26, was an exciting and nerve-wracking day. I brought Gracelyn, Josiah, and Eliana to Bonnie and Troy's house and unloaded all their things. I went over Gracelyn's health needs again with Bonnie and Troy, leaving them with a long, handwritten instruction sheet. I stayed and had a short visit with them. When it was time to leave, the kids were happily playing and hardly said goodbye to me. It was emotional for me, as this was to be the longest I had ever been away from them, but it reassured me that they felt at home there. I knew that they would be well taken care of.

I drove Mackenzie to Mark's parents' place and picked up Deanne, who had flown in from B.C. the night before. Deanne came with me to drop Jonah off at the Zingers' in Edmonton. Once Jonah was out of the van, the atmosphere changed and the reality of the trip pressed in. It was an odd combination of fear and elation. I didn't quite know what to do with myself without the kids. I suddenly had the freedom not to have to worry about them, as I knew that each of my kids here in Canada was safe and that both of my kids in Ethiopia were safe, too.

Deanne and I chatted excitedly about the next day and headed for a mall to do the last of our shopping. I needed to buy myself some jeans, as the ones I had were falling off me. The combination of stress and busyness and the difficulty I had encountered with food in the days when I'd worried about Elijah and Sedaya going without had taken a toll on my body. In the less than two weeks since the bankruptcy fiasco had begun, I'd lost more than eleven pounds, which on my small five-foot frame was significant. All of my clothes were baggy.

Deanne and I had a great time shopping, although we accomplished little. I felt light and carefree. There was nothing left to be done and I would soon be on my way to hold my children. It looked as though all the work I had done advocating for their entry into Canada was going to pay off. In just two short weeks, our family would be together, complete. When Deanne and I stopped for supper on the way back, I was able to eat without guilt. I was able to taste the food, to enjoy it.

Deanne and I were up for most of the night. We went online and booked our seats on the flights where that was possible. We did laundry, folded clothes, and put them away, as I didn't want to come home to piles of laundry in addition to what would be coming in the bags from the nine of us. I put the first items of clothing in Elijah and Sedaya's dresser drawers and smiled as I hung a few dresses for my new daughter in her closet. I now believed that the day would come when I would be tucking them into bed here in these bedrooms.

Deanne and I rearranged our bags so that everything important would fit. We repeatedly took them to the bathroom scale to check that they were under the weight allowances. With some reshuffling, we were able to fit everything in. We ensured that we had our tickets and passports at the ready. Deanne and I listened endlessly to the Amharic language CD. I was surprised by how much had started to sink in for me already and felt a bit more confident about my ability to communicate with the kids once we arrived.

We tidied up what we could in the house to get it ready for our homecoming. It was a comfort to know that while we were in Ethiopia, my mom was going to come and prepare the kids' bedrooms. In the end, while we were away, many people would come to help with painting and decorating the rooms, assembling beds, buying and washing sheets, and stocking our kitchen with some basic grocery items. By the time we got home, all of our kids' rooms, not just Elijah and Sedaya's, looked like they had been transformed by Extreme Makeover Home Edition! Peel Monkey, the vinyl wall art division of my brother's graphic design company, made custom surface decals for each of the rooms. What a blessing to come home to!

It was 3:00 in the morning when Deanne and I finally went to sleep. We weren't concerned about the time, as we knew that there would be plenty of opportunity to sleep on the planes over the next few days. We set our alarm and slept right through it! I had been waking up early without being able to go back to sleep for more than a week. On the day that I actually needed to be awake, on the day that would begin the most important journey of my life, I slept through the alarm!

Thankfully, God had already made backup arrangements, so we were able to get to the airport in time. We had made plans with my brother-in-law John to pick us up for the flight, but we had initially gotten the flight time wrong. The night before, we realized that we had made a mistake, so we left John a message asking him to come an hour later than we had previously arranged. Fortunately for us, though, he hadn't listened to the message, so he arrived early and banged on the door until he woke us.

We weren't late for the flight, but were considerably frazzled upon our arrival! The feeling I'd had just a week before when taking Mark to the airport was of such uncertainty. Just one week later, so much had changed. I was almost positive that we were going to be allowed to bring Elijah and Sedaya home with us. When I boarded that first flight from Edmonton to Toronto, it felt like I was taking the first step to bringing my babies home. What a feeling!

The airport in Toronto was overwhelming. I had never been in such a large airport and we had to transfer to a different terminal to board our international flight. We had a hard time finding anyone who could answer our questions about where to go. I felt lost and a bit scared, like a small town girl plunked down in Times Square. There were many hours between our flights, and the hectic pace of the preceding days began to wear on me. The adrenaline that had carried me for two weeks was tapering off now that the peak of the crisis was over, and I felt weary.

The trip from Toronto to Dubai was fourteen hours, none of which I slept. I made every effort, but with so much excitement and nervousness built up in me, rest simply wouldn't come. I was able to watch movies and read, but I found myself distracted by thoughts of Elijah and Sedaya, and of what I would find when I got to Ethiopia. I had dreamed of this country for so long, and now that the time to see it was here, I was anxious about how it would affect me.

I was worried most about how I would react to seeing up close the eyes of orphans and of men and women in distress. I need not have worried. There is so much suffering in Ethiopia, yet there is also much joy. The country taught me more about love and joy and God than I could have thought possible. It would come to be harder to leave it and to take my children from it than I can express. Ethiopia was beautiful in its countryside, its people, its culture, and its heart.

Arriving in the airport in Dubai was like landing on a futuristic planet. The closest thing I can relate to the opulence that surrounded me is a Las Vegas hotel, with its massive ceilings and pillars and ornate detailing. There were fountains, mirrors, lights, and music. The ambiance was formal. The grandeur was beyond my scope of experience. The flowing white robes and headpieces worn by the personnel working in the airport added to the illusion. It was obvious that we were no longer in Canada! The wave of heat that hit us when we walked outside the airport terminal was humid and gave the impression of walking out into a giant sauna.

As we drove from the airport to the nearby hotel, I wished that I could see more of Dubai. My Auntie Judy and Uncle Ken had lived in the United Arab Emirates for five years a few years before and some of their stories came flooding back as we drove by the impressive sights. Even the buildings under construction were amazing. Seeing just this tiny bit made me curious about the people, the customs, and the country.

By the time we checked into the hotel, which the airline had provided, it was too late in the evening to see any of Dubai, so Deanne and I walked next door to a Mexican restaurant. The irony of eating Mexican food in a Middle Eastern country was not lost on me, but traditional UAE cuisine wasn't available at that hour. We enjoyed ourselves immensely and talked mostly about our expectations for the following day. There was a palpable excitement in the air.

I was once again so thankful to have Deanne with me. I was able to have fun and feel more relaxed and confident than I would have had I been flying alone. Our hotel room was reminiscent of an army barracks, but it served its purpose for the night. We were so cold, though. We couldn't figure out how to turn down the air conditioning, and with the high humidity, things were damp. We had to laugh about how chilled to the bone we were feeling in the hottest place we had ever visited. Outside, it was well above forty degrees Celsius! We got very little sleep, as there was no clock in the room and neither of us had a watch. We kept worrying about oversleeping again and missing our flight in the morning.

I was a bundle of nerves, knowing that only a three-hour flight separated me from my children.

s i x t e e n

BY 4:00 A.M., I WAS SHOWERED, DRESSED, AND PACKED, AND I HAD FINISHED reading the novel I had brought in my carry-on. A quick breakfast and shuttle ride found us back at the posh Dubai airport. We perused the expensive shops and Deanne got herself a Starbucks coffee… some things are the same, no matter where in the world you are!

I was so nervous about how the kids would react to me. Would they be happy to see me, or would they be wary of my intrusion? Would they like me, or would they wish they had gotten a different mom? How would they adjust to life in Canada, and life in our family? Would they wish I were prettier or more fun? Would they be scared of me? How were their hearts adjusting to all the changes?

I said another prayer for them, asking God to prepare their hearts even now. I loved them so much already, but I needed to remind myself that this didn't mean they would love me instantly. I also prepared myself for the chance that after being with Mark for a week already, they would have bonded with him and might resent my presence. The thought scared me. I also wondered how I would get along with Ethiopia, the land of my son and daughter's birth. I'm an indoors kind of girl and not very adventurous. I'm afraid of heights and mice, and I'm squeamish when it comes to food, so this trip was way outside of my comfort zone.

With less than an hour to go before boarding the plane that would take me to my children, the situation felt surreal. It had yet to fully sink in that I was going to fulfill a dream that had begun so many years before. So much had led to that moment—mounds of paperwork, invasive home studies, background checks, hopes, anticipation, prayers, months and years of waiting, fundraisers, saving, debt, excitement, and dreams. There was also the joy of learning who our new family members would be and planning. Then there was the news of Imagine's bankruptcy and the chaotic, sometimes heart-wrenching moments of the past two weeks. It had all brought us here: Mark, already with our children in Addis, eagerly awaiting the arrival of reinforcements, and me, sitting on a yellow chair next to Deanne in the United Arab Emirates, half a world from home, knowing that from this day forward, my life would never be the same.

The time from Dubai to Addis Ababa was short. Before I knew it, I could see the landing strip. I knew that Mark and my kids were just below, waiting for me. I was grinning from ear to ear, my stomach doing flip-flops. I was right there. I could see the city. I could see the airport. I was about to finally hold my son and my daughter. I was so close.

We had started our descent, and then I felt the plane pull up slightly. Warning bells went off in my mind. At first, I chided myself for being paranoid. I assumed that in my excitement, I was just imagining a worst-case scenario, but soon it became clear that we were not descending. Due to weather, the plane couldn't land, though from my clear view of the airport, it seemed that we could. As we circled the city unable to land, the song that had brought me such comfort a week earlier came to mind again: "Savior, He can move the mountains. Our God is mighty to save. He is mighty to save." It gave me a small amount of comfort to believe that a God who can move mountains and conquer the grave, and had gotten me this far, could surely get me from where I was to my children.

When it still wasn't clear to land and we were running low on fuel, we rerouted to Djibouti to refuel. Djibouti wasn't a country that had ever beckoned to me. It wasn't one that I had a desire to see, and certainly not one where I wanted to visit, with my arms aching for my children. The landing strip in Djibouti was dirt and had small dry twigs poking up through it. The view was dreary. I was very quiet in my seat while we waited on a dusty tarmac in this small African country that wasn't our intended destination. I fought tears and waves of crushing disappointment. Logically, I reasoned that within an hour, we should be back in Ethiopia, but I knew with an assurance that I couldn't pinpoint that I would not be able to lay eyes on my beautiful son and daughter that day.

We passed over Addis Ababa again, circled again, and still didn't land. It seemed at the moment like a cruel joke. After all we had gone through in the past weeks to get to here, to be so close and not be able to be with them was gutting. Irrationally, I wanted to go into the cockpit and beg the pilots to land. I stayed seated. We flew to Entebbe, Uganda, a country even further away from my children than Djibouti had been. Our landing was rough. At one point, we even started to veer off the runway. I felt no fear, though, only numbness at the turn the day had taken.

We were ushered off the plane and told that we were getting off so that they could clean the plane, but it was obvious from the whispering going on among the crew that there was a much bigger issue than snack wrappers on the floor. We were taken by bus to the terminal, where we were herded like cattle into a glass-paneled holding room. There was no air conditioning, no water, and it was so hot. Sweat trickled down my back.

After three hours, people were crying and demanding answers. Hours and hours went by with no response. A kind American couple who ran a mission in Uganda allowed me to use their cell phone to try to call Mark, but none of us could figure out how to properly dial the country code. I found out later that when using a cell phone, the prefix is different.

I was worried about how the kids may be affected by this. Mark was working hard to establish trust with them and he had assured them that they were going to the airport to meet their mommy. What would they think when I wasn't there? I later found out that Mark had made three separate trips to the airport, each time enduring Sedaya's car sickness during the drives and having to go through security just to get inside, and then each time having to return to the hotel with upset kids and without me.

I was numb and worried, and I felt cheated. I was exhausted. The word "disappointment" didn't even come close to describing what I felt during those long hours. I was at times scared, as no airline officials would tell us what was going on and there began to be talk of putting us in a hotel in Uganda for the rest of the night. We had departed Dubai in the morning for a three-hour flight to Ethiopia, and it was now dark outside. From time to time, the Gilligan's Island theme song got stuck in my head, the one about the three-hour tour!

As I sat in the sweltering room, I was struck by the irony that Mark, the adventure seeker and experienced traveler, had arrived in Addis Ababa without incident, whereas I, the reluctant traveler, was now in my second African country of the day, neither of which was the one I had set out for!

The airport staff was unsure what to do with us. To allow us into the regular airport would have required visas, so we continued to be confined to the sweltering holding room. After being without food or drink for many hours, they decided to give us vouchers for donuts and drinks in the nearby cafeteria. They formed lines to check our passports and hand us the food tickets. I wasn't able to eat anything, as my nerves were fried, but it was great to get out of that room.

These unexpected detours made me all the more grateful to have Deanne with me. I would have been so afraid if I had been by myself. In one of the lineups, we met an Australian family who were also on their way to adopt siblings in Ethiopia. We were able to chat with them and compare notes, which made the experience seem a bit more normal.

Eventually, we came to hear that two or more of the plane's tires had popped on our landing in Djibouti, which explained the rocky landing in Entebbe. They were attempting to repair the plane, but they weren't sure how many more hours this would take. Logically, I knew that I was closer to the kids than I had been a week ago, but it felt in that moment like I would never get to Ethiopia. I felt like I was further away from them than I had been when I was back in Canada. I wanted to curl up in a ball on the floor and have a good cry!

I was mostly silent in the hours that we were in Entebbe. Being too quiet isn't a description that normally applies to me, as I'm very talkative by nature. I spent some of the time convincing myself that I would get to Ethiopia eventually, and I spent the rest of the time praying. As the hours stretched on, I felt more and more disconnected from the anticipation I had felt that morning. I tried to have perspective by thinking about the mothers in the room who had young children with them or the elderly who had a much worse time with the heat and the long wait than I did.

The three-hour flight stretched to seventeen hours of waiting, so by the time we landed in Ethiopia, it was the following day. I had been able to call Mark once we reboarded the plane, and he and I fought about him coming back to the airport with the kids. I had so anticipated seeing the faces of my kids and Mark there to greet me. I begged him to come. He had endured a day as exhausting as mine, and the kids were finally asleep in their beds at the hotel. He had no intention of waking them and making another journey back to the airport.

After Deanne and I finally landed and deplaned in Addis Ababa, we stood in line to get our visas, collect our bags, and clear security. When we walked out to the main area, it was nearly impossible for me to hold back my tears when we were met by a driver instead of Mark, Elijah, and Sedaya. I had a lump in my throat the size of a plum during the drive, and all efforts at making conversation with the driver resulted in stinging tears.

The driver was very kind and he stated that after a day of so much travel and confusion, I must be too exhausted to talk! It was dark and I wasn't able to take in much of Ethiopia, so I didn't form much of a first impression apart from our friendly and compassionate driver and guide, who did his best to put me at ease. The minute I got into the hotel room, I went into the bathroom and bawled. The acute emotions of the past days and weeks caught up with me and I broke down. It was devastating not to be met by the kids after such a horrendous day. It was one of the most disappointing feelings of my life. For three years, I had dreamed of the moment I would meet my kids for the first time. After not sleeping for over twenty-five hours and hardly eating all day, I was finally in Ethiopia. But here I was, crumpled in a heap on a cold bathroom floor, sobbing. This was not the image I had pictured.

Mark was less than impressed at my dash into the bathroom of the hotel room and was hurt when he came in and found me crying. Leading up to my arrival, he'd been having a hard time with the kids and was counting down the minutes until his reinforcements arrived. When our plane was delayed, his day became a nightmare of navigating the streets and airport of Addis Ababa with two cranky children. The kids already didn't trust him, and it did nothing to improve the situation when he kept telling them that they were going to go and pick up this elusive "mommy" person and then not being able to keep his word.

We were both exhausted and emotional, and blame was being thrown around freely in the small hotel bathroom that night. Mark informed me that I had no idea the hell he had been going through with the kids and that he was worried about what the decision to add them would do to our family. He told me that he loved them already, but that they were incredibly difficult and defiant. His words stung. When he told me that the next day that I would see what he'd been dealing with, part of me thought that surely I would be able to manage them better, that my love would win them over.

What a surprise I had in store for me! I acted like a spoiled child who didn't get her way and wouldn't budge on my assertion that he should have known how important it was for me to be there when I got off the plane. After coming to no resolution, Mark went out to have a visit with Deanne and I stayed and sobbed out my feelings.

When I had cried out all the pain of the past two weeks, I got up and went into the main room. I was able to go up to where Elijah and Sedaya were sleeping and watch them. It pained me not to wake them, but I knew that they'd had a hard day, too, and needed to sleep. They were sharing a huge Queen-size bed, their little bodies almost lost in a sea of white bedding.

Seeing them safe and knowing that they were in our care was a balm. It helped ease some of the disappointment I had felt at not being able to meet them right away. They were so much more beautiful than I had imagined and none of the worry and trauma that they had endured in their young lives showed in their slumbered state. Watching them was the comfort I needed to be able to settle into my own sleep for a few hours.

First thing in the morning, I was up and showering. I was nervous, excited, and the light of day brought reality to being so close to my children. I made no effort to be quiet when I was getting ready, hoping to wake the kids up, but they slept through everything.

Sedaya was the first to wake up. I sat down on the edge of the bed and said hello in Amharic. It felt surreal to be introducing myself to my own daughter! I could tell that she recognized me from the pictures she had been shown and I got a sliver of a smile. Her smile widened considerably when I gave her the Cabbage Patch Doll I had brought for her. She and I changed the doll's clothes a few times, but exchanged few words because of the language barrier and Elijah still being asleep right next to us. In the few pictures we had been sent, Sedaya didn't look like a particularly attractive child, but in person she was so beautiful, her eyes bright and her smile a bit mischievous! Elijah slept through it all until Sedaya decided to wake him up, excited to show him her new baby doll.

Elijah's reaction to me was very reserved at first, but I could see the relief on his face that I was there and that I was real. It was a wonderful moment. Elijah didn't want to get out of the bed until I brought him his pants, something he communicated to me by repeating the Amharic word for pants until Mark rescued me by interpreting! Even once he had his pants on, he was very quiet, head down, stealing glances at me from time to time. He livened up when I showed him the View Master I had brought for him and began talking rapidly, mostly in Amharic, about the cars he could see in the pictures. As the three of us played together, Mark and Deanne slipped out of the room for a coffee and I was by myself in a strange country with two children I had never met but who were my own.

Nothing could have felt more natural.

seventeen

MY FIRST DAY IN ETHIOPIA WAS A BIT LIKE BEING THROWN INTO THE DEEP end of a wave pool without a life jacket. Mark had warned me that the kids were having a hard time adjusting. Their transition was proving to be difficult and I got my first taste of it that morning with a christening of tantrums and tears.

The first meltdown I witnessed happened over a pair of shoes. Sedaya wanted to wear Elijah's flip-flops, but of all the sizes of shoes we'd brought for him, those were really the only ones that fit him, so he needed to wear them. She refused to put her shoes on and wailed, hit, and kicked me as I tried to get them on her feet. First, I tried reasoning with her. Obviously, reasoning with a distraught four-year-old who doesn't understand a word you're saying isn't an effective strategy! I then decided that maybe it was best to be strict in order to set a precedent and explained, using a few words and gestures, that if she kicked me again, she would have to sit in the bathroom.

In retrospect, this may not have been the best strategy either, as she came unglued and came after me with fists flying, her face full of what I perceived to be rage. I now recognize it for what it was: fear. I decided to follow through on my threat and gave her her first "timeout." Part of me was trying to prove to Mark that these children were not impossible to manage and that they just needed some structure, for us to set some behavioral expectations.

Looking back, I wonder if perhaps the jetlag was messing with my head! The timeout only made Sedaya absolutely panic and she flung herself around the room, screaming hysterically and trying to escape out the main door. By this point, Elijah was refusing to put his shoes on as well and I slowly began to have a window into what the past week must have been like for Mark!

We had to quickly get the kids ready, take them to breakfast, and pack for the day before our driver arrived. Somehow we managed to get out the door on time, but not before tears were shed by almost all of us. I can't remember exactly how things were resolved, but I do know that Sedaya eventually agreed to let me put shoes on her feet and carry her down to the lobby.

Mark and another adoptive family he had met at the guest house the week before had made plans for us to go visit Faya Orphanage. Faya was the orphanage that we had held our first fundraiser for. Because of this, it was close to my heart. It had taken many late nights of baking to raise the $700 for Faya. So often, as North Americans, we write a check or attend a fundraiser for something that we've never had the chance to see firsthand, to help people we've never met, so this was a unique occasion. I was excited to have the opportunity to go there, but still tired after my stressful days of travel and my three hours of restless sleep.

Had we known about my flight not arriving until the wee hours of the morning, Mark wouldn't have planned the trek for that day. I loaded two bags up with some of the donations I had brought and we got into the van and went to pick up the other adoptive family.

I'd only met Arnica, the adoptive mother, online prior to this. It therefore felt very surreal to be meeting her and her mom, along with her beautiful twin girls, in another country. I had seen pictures of Arnica's girls in emails, but now they were in a van with me, talking to my children, who I had also only known from pictures in emails.

Arnica had been one of the first parents to hop aboard a plane when the announcement of the agency's bankruptcy came. She and her husband had gotten their referral of their twin girls in October 2008, but it had taken eight months and seven court dates for the girls to legally become their daughters. Understandably, Arnica and her husband hadn't wanted to take any chances on losing the girls, so Arnica had packed her bags to come immediately.

Faya was located in Nazret, about a two-hour drive from the capital. As we drove, I was struck by the beauty of Ethiopia, especially the countryside. As it was the rainy season, there was lush green scenery, something I hadn't pictured when I thought of Ethiopia. There were so many things to see that were completely outside the realm of my experience. My senses could barely take it all in! There were cows, oxen, goats, chickens, sheep, horses, and donkeys right on or beside the road. I saw women with babies strapped to their backs, small children hauling bundles of wood wider than they were tall, roadside stands with meat swarming with flies, busy markets alive with color, people plowing manually, and little boys herding cattle with whips. We passed by a somber funeral procession. What struck me about the procession was how ordinary it was for the villagers. No one even gave it a second glance, indicating to me that this must be a common sight.

As we drove past, I caught a glimpse of a young boy using a tattered, frayed rope to skip with in the ditch. The image stayed with me. He looked so happy.

One of the most noticeable things was that there were so many half-completed buildings. Scaffolding sat empty. Some huge projects seemed to have amazing architectural design but were left unfinished, abandoned. The money had run out, but the hollow shapes remained, a haunting reminder of what could have been. The incomplete buildings seemed to mirror so much of what the country had become, a people filled with hope and promise and potential, but without enough money to fulfill their dreams, even if their dreams were as simple as feeding their children.

When we arrived at Faya, we were met by the director and taken to see the home and meet the children. "Home" is the best word I can use to describe Faya, because the caregivers' love and care for the children was evident. Though the furniture was sparse and the home simple, it was clean and well cared for. Next to the combined sitting, kitchen, and dining area, there were beds and cribs to sleep five children in a space no larger than the smallest bedroom in our house back home. There were other sleeping rooms off the narrow corridor, and there was a small office.

When we arrived, the children were coloring at a long table on the porch. They followed us into the small fenced backyard. The kids were so happy to see us, and they were thrilled just to have us play simple games with them like jump rope, catch, and clapping sing-songs. It took so little to bring them great joy. I was able to hold a three-month-old baby girl, and when she smiled up at me, it was difficult to fight the urge to find a way to bring her home, too. At three months old, her story was already so sad and I didn't want that to define who she would become. The thought of stowing her in my carry-on crossed my mind!

There are many children waiting to come into this small orphanage, but there isn't enough room or money to make it possible for Faya to accept them. Caring for babies is especially expensive because of the higher costs of formula and medical care. It was humbling to see how grateful the staff was for the donations we brought with us. The director started pulling out the clothes we had brought and immediately called a little boy into the room to see if any of the pants fit him. The pants he was wearing were visibly too small, but as she held up the pants we had brought it became clear that none of them were his size, either. I felt helpless, standing and watching the exchange as

I saw his excitement at the possibility and then glimpsed his momentary disappointment before he ran back out to play.

In that moment, I wished so much that I had brought more, had brought every clothing size and item. It was ridiculous to stand there with nothing to give this boy when my kids at home had drawers full of clothes. Here, the children were wearing anything that fit, boys wearing pink ruffled shirts without complaint, which was such a contrast to Canadian society where kids wore the latest name brand fashion, and in gender-specific colors.

The director was so appreciative of our donations of clothing, shoes, medication, and money, and yet I felt like it was too little. I was reassured somewhat with the knowledge that Arnica and her husband were going to be returning to Faya sometime in the coming weeks. With the money that had been collected across Canada to care for the kids in the Transition Home, they would purchase large items for Faya such as bunk beds, mattresses, dressers, and a couch, as well as formula and teff flour. Once Yamana Gold had stepped in with their huge financial donation, the money collected was no longer needed, and a vote determined that the money would go to help Faya.

At Faya, we had a traditional Ethiopian coffee ceremony. It was significant and meaningful for me. In the past, when adoptive families had gone to pick up their children at Imagine's Transition Home, they had been given a traditional coffee ceremony and it was something I had looked forward to. When Mark had gone to pick up our kids, I hadn't been there to experience it. In all the chaos of the bankruptcy, coffee ceremonies were pretty low on the priority list, so Mark didn't get to experience it, either. Having one here, at this wonderful orphanage where I could so clearly see that God's work was being done, felt perfect. I'm not a coffee drinker, but the small cup of delicious coffee was strong, freshly roasted, and loaded with sugar. The smell of the beans filled the room and the sweetness of what I had thought would be a bitter drink was a welcome surprise.

The kids loved our digital cameras and a few of them took the cameras around the yard to take photos of their friends. The kids laughed like crazy when I took pictures of their shoes. I'm not sure why it made them giggle, but before I knew it, they were all gathered round, asking for me to take a photo of their *chowmas*! Mark kicked a ball around with the boys, and at one point he had kids climbing all over him! I laughed when I later saw a little boy walking through the yard wearing Mark's glasses. I handed out a few of the small toys I'd brought for each of the kids and was amazed at the level of their thankfulness. Again, I found myself wishing I had brought more.

Our own kids were very quiet, and Sedaya especially was quite weepy. Both kids seemed anxious and on edge. We had gotten our driver to explain to them that we were only going to visit the other kids and that they would be coming back with us, but I think they felt insecure and worried that we might have brought them to the orphanage to leave them there. Elijah and Sedaya had already been through three moves in the past five months and permanency was not a familiar concept to them.

Deanne skipped rope with the girls and tried to learn their clapping games. Her heart was captured by one boy in particular, and it seemed that the feeling was mutual. Watching Deanne interact with the kids was magical. Deanne was just living in the moment, not caring about anything in the world except the here and now as she poured her love and Jesus' love into these kids for the few hours she was with them. I have never seen her look so free, so joyful, so alive! Being at Faya was intoxicating. I felt like I was a small part of something bigger and I never wanted to leave.

That day, I saw joy in so many forms, a gift that these children—who had so little else—seemed to have in abundance. Joy radiated from their shining eyes, shone in their faces, glowed in their smiles, and echoed in their laughter. I saw true joy for perhaps the first time, and it was magnificent! I saw Jesus at Faya that day.

eighteen

AS WE WERE LEAVING FAYA, MARK BOUGHT SOME ROASTED PEANUTS FROM a man on the street. It cost him one Birr per handful and we would later regret not filling bags with the aromatic crunchy treat. They were wonderful and helped abate our growing hunger.

Arnica, her mom, her girls, Mark, Deanne, Elijah, Sedaya, the driver, our guide, Faya's director, and I went for lunch at the African Safari Lodge. The grounds were lush and breathtaking and the outdoor restaurant was like an oasis from the dusty roads. We ate a savory meal of traditional Ethiopian cuisine and I felt myself relaxing and having fun. The kids devoured the *injera*, *doro wat*, *tibs*, and *shiro* and loved their *Mirindas* (orange soda). I could see that they were already starting to bond with Mark when I saw Elijah copying exactly what Mark was doing at the table! It was fun to listen to the banter between our kids and Arnica's, and I'm sure it was amusing to the others at the table to hear the Canadians trying to communicate with the kids. Arnica had been there long enough to learn some key phrases and I was happy to log them into my memory.

The drive back to Addis Ababa was again filled with stops for the kids to go to the bathroom or for Sedaya to throw up, though her motion sickness didn't always give enough notice for us to pull over in time. I made a mental note to begin carrying bags with us whenever we took her in a vehicle.

Traffic in the city was like nothing I had ever seen. There were no street lights or signs and much of the right of way was determined by the looks that drivers gave each other. Simple gestures or the raising of an eyebrow could signify communication between drivers. There seemed to be some unspoken rules of the road, although those also appeared to be fluid. Our throats were thick with the overpowering exhaust fumes, at times heavy enough to create a feeling of nausea. Pedestrians crossed the streets anywhere and the vans, cars, and busses shared the uneven roads with the donkeys and horses and carts, making travel very interesting! Mark equated it with the Indiana Jones ride at Disneyland and commented that our older boys would have enjoyed the adventure of it.

Mark hadn't been able to pick up much Amharic, so pointing and gesturing were his main method of conversation with the kids. Much of the week before I arrived had been filled with tantrumming, due to Elijah and Sedaya's fears, misunderstandings, and inability to communicate with Mark.

I was therefore determined to learn as much Amharic as I could during my short stay in Ethiopia. It quickly became apparent that many of the phrases I'd taught myself before coming wouldn't be useful. I could ask "How are you?" but unless their response was "good" or "bad," I had no idea what they were saying! The first time I asked one of them, I felt quite proud of myself for pronouncing the question correctly, but when I got a five-word response, I was left open-mouthed and silent.

Amharic has been influenced over the years by Arabic and Italian. Although I have no familiarity with Arabic, Italian and French are both rooted in Latin. I grew up speaking French fluently, so this gave me a starting point. I took notes of all the Amharic words I learned. I also asked for translation for phrases that I found myself needing to use with the kids, such as "It's okay," "Later," "Wait," and "Come." I had already memorized all the words relating to bathrooms, which came in very handy. Amharic has slight differences when you are speaking to a boy as opposed to a girl, or for if you are speaking to more than one person. Because we had both a boy and a girl and there were two of them, I had to learn all possible versions of each of the words I wanted to use.

One day, when Mark had gone to the embassy to pick up the kids' visas, Sedaya locked herself in the bathroom and couldn't unlock the door. Her screaming upset Elijah, who buried his head in a suitcase and cried. Deanne and I frantically looked up the words for "open" and "turn" in the Amharic-English dictionary we had purchased in the Toronto airport. We never were able to pronounce them effectively enough to get our point across. We had to get a lady on the cleaning staff to open the door using a special key. We also asked her to explain to the kids what had happened so that Elijah wouldn't think I had locked his sister in there!

The day after Deanne and I arrived, we got word that our visas had been issued! The first time Mark went to the embassy to pick up the kids' visas, he had been unsuccessful, but a few hours later he received a call letting him know that the right person had arrived. He went back and finally returned with the facilitation visas that would allow Elijah and Sedaya into Canada. When Mark got back from the embassy, I was anxious to see what we had been fighting for nineteen days for. I laughed when I saw the small sticker in each of their passports. One sticker had been standing in the way of their homecoming, and now that obstacle had been defeated! We'd received our miracle!

On the morning of August 1, Mark, Deanne, and I took the kids and went to visit AHOPE, an American-founded orphanage for HIV-positive babies and children. I brought two bags of shoes and medicine, and again I found myself wishing that I had brought more. We had the privilege of spending time in the baby room, where we held tiny babes. The youngest was only eighteen days old, named Setota, which means "gift," a fitting name for this wee precious girl. Mark had been holding a little boy who I guessed to be about a year old. He continually came back to Mark to be picked up and giggled when Mark made silly faces at him.

The baby room had brightly painted wooden cupboards that ran the length of three of the walls. Atop them were wooden dividers, and a baby slept in each section. In this way, they could maximize space and fit almost a dozen babies in the small room.

I had a one-month-old baby girl in my arms who looked up at me with such big, bright eyes. I thought of all the promise and potential her life had and prayed that she would be able to fulfill the plans God had for her future. We were told that although this young baby had initially tested positive for HIV after being born to a mother living with the disease, she was now testing negative. My heart rejoiced for her and I gave silent praise at the glimmer of hope amid stories of such tragedy.

Some of the babies already had lesions on their faces, but it took only a look into their eyes to see past the lesions straight through to their smiles. Being there and holding those children, I felt no hesitation or fear about their HIV. I saw only babies, deserving of love and a family. Already, they had been born in a country where their chances of reaching adulthood were among the lowest in the world. On top of that, they had been born with a serious disease and were living in an orphanage. There were so many factors against them, and yet in their spirits I could sense joy, resilience, and a willingness to love. It was a beautiful experience.

Mark and Deanne went out with Elijah and Sedaya to see the home where the preschoolers lived, but before I left the house the babies were in, I passed by a small room where a thin girl about the age of eleven was lying in bed. I asked her caregiver if it was okay for me to go in and she smiled and beckoned me inside. It was obvious that AIDS had taken a toll on this young girl's life. She was blind and it was evident that she was dying.

At first, I felt like I was intruding but when I said, "Selam," her face lit up and she reached out for me. I took her hands in mine and sat on the bed. I gave her a small plastic bracelet and she was overjoyed when I put it on her wrist. In that moment, I wished so much that I had more to give her. She was so beautiful and happy, despite her circumstances. She was excited by the small ball I pressed into her palm and tossed it up and caught it repeatedly. She and I didn't share the same language or the same background, but we were both children of the same God.

We shared a precious short time together that I will never forget. In those minutes with a dying child, I saw nothing but life. I sang to the girl whose name I'll never know, and when she said, "Thank you," a lump formed in my throat. How could I ever thank her for the gift she had given me?

I had seen so many pictures of Ethiopia and the orphans there, and I had watched videos about the poverty in the country, but I had never expected it to affect me the way it did. I could never have prepared for being there. The smell of dirt, manure, pollution, and urine hung thick and heavy, and these smells made what I was seeing real. The other difference was the humanity of being up close, of touching the women and children, of looking into their eyes and knowing that there was only one reason that they were at risk for starvation, disease, and death and I was not. I was born in Canada and they were born in Ethiopia. The unfairness of it stopped me at times, making me feel powerless and weak.

Some of what I saw in Addis Ababa made me want to turn away. I was disgusted with myself for wanting to avert my eyes from what I was seeing, because I should not have had that option. I forced myself to see, to take it all in. I looked into the eyes of mothers who were begging for money for food to feed their children. I saw the children living on the streets, donning clothing that had been worn to rags. I saw the crippled fathers who were unable to provide even the simplest needs for their families. I forced myself to feel, not to turn off my emotions, so that I would never forget, so that I would go home to my comfortable life in Canada and do whatever I could to make a difference for these worthy people. I knew that I was forever changed.

nineteen

MARK AND I WANTED TO BRING LITTLE BITS OF ETHIOPIA BACK HOME WITH us so that Elijah and Sedaya would have treasures to remember their home country by. We went to a pottery co-op run by women and purchased intricately hand-painted souvenirs. Sadly, we hadn't brought bubble wrap, as others had suggested to us, and they now sit on our bedroom dresser in pieces.

We went to a weaving house and watched as scarves were woven. We bought several to bring home. One is used now as a table runner for special occasions. There was a wonderful store that sold items made by disabled Ethiopians where we got wooden puzzles, kitchen linens, toys, and a hand-stitched purse. Since Ethiopia is known for its coffee, we stopped to buy coffee beans and grounds. The wood carvings we bought will be lovely keepsakes for Elijah and Sedaya when they are older, and we made sure to buy an ornament for our Christmas tree and for theirs when they are grown. Finally, we bought traditional Ethiopian outfits and necklaces for each of our kids.

In the market, streets were lined with makeshift tents and vendors selling all manner of goods. As we were leaving on our first visit there, I handed out toy vehicles to some of the boys and created a bit of a mob outside our van as we were rushed by more than ten boys hoping to receive a toy or money from us. I handed out as many as I had, but there were more urgent hands reaching in and nothing left to give them. There were shoeshine boys at the market who lived on the street, and one of them captured my attention because his eyes were deadened. He had lost hope. Nothing brought a smile to his face. As he went through the motions of earning his living, I carefully watched his face for some sign of life, but saw none.

We returned to the same market a few days later and he was there again with no hint of spark in his eyes. I wanted to take him into my arms and tell him that he was worth loving, that God had not forgotten him. I wish I had. My own insecurities about looking ridiculous talked me out of it under the guise of not wanting to scare him. I wish now that I had taken the risk.

Driving through the capital city on my third day in Ethiopia, I was entranced by the mosaic of mismatched colors which together created a unified art. There were shelters made of sticks, corrugated tin, and brightly hued tarps. We saw a sheep market, beautiful flowering trees, more donkeys and chickens in the street, and a large gathering for men teaching about AIDS.

There was so much to see as we navigated the narrow streets and grew accustomed to the sounds of car horns. Sitting outside small shacks, women washed garments in the brown water of their basins, hanging them up to dry. Women and children carried large bundles of wood on their backs, the bundles often wider than the bearers were tall. Donkeys also carried loads and knew where to go on their own. The sounds, smells, and buildings were all so different from home.

Later, back in our room, I lay on the bed looking through an Amharic phrasebook with Elijah snuggled up next to me, his hand resting on my chest. When I would pronounce a word wrong, he would correct me. If it was a word that he felt was important, he would point at my piece of paper, wanting me to write it down for future reference. As my Amharic came along, the kids grew somewhat less frustrated. However, the more I learned, the more they thought I knew, so at times they would say, "Mommy," followed by a full sentence or two in Amharic. I was a fast learner, but not that fast! The kids seemed to appreciate my efforts, at least.

There were power outages two or three times a week during out stay. On my fourth day, we took a taxi in an attempt to go to the Natural History Museum, which Arnica had told us her kids really enjoyed. The driver took us to the wrong museum and, in a funny twist, that day was a no-power day so we toured the university's Institute of Ethiopian Studies completely in the dark! It made us appreciative for the electricity that we took for granted back home.

Culturally, Ethiopian children are largely cared for by the community as a whole. It was a good thing that others had warned me that Ethiopians will just come over, pick up your kids, and walk off with them. I would have panicked had I not been prepared for this. We found the Ethiopians we encountered friendly towards us and caring towards our children. People in the street or in restaurants would approach us to thank us for coming to adopt the kids. Many of them remarked that they had heard of Ethiopian babies being adopted by Americans and Canadians, but that they were so thankful we were taking older children and giving them a chance at a better life. They would tell Elijah and Sedaya how lucky they were to be going to Canada, and also tell them to be good for their new parents. To us, they would say, "May God bless you for what you are doing."

This kindness was very humbling, because here they were, as a country, allowing us to take away two of their most valuable natural resources. During the first few days, I would explain that we were the lucky ones, that we were honored to be able to adopt these beautiful children. This was met with confusion and argument, so I learned to accept their words with only a smile and a thank you ("Amisaganalo").

The driver and guide we used for much of our stay in Ethiopia were employees of Imagine Adoption who had lost their jobs with the bankruptcy. I was keenly aware that after the wave of parents coming to pick up the remainder of the kids in the Transition Home had gone, their livelihood would be gone as well. It angered me to know that the greed of one or two Canadians had caused so much suffering for so many.

twenty

ETHIOPIA IS A COUNTRY RICH IN HISTORY AND CULTURE AND WE HAD PLANNED to see more of it. Mark had hoped to be able to travel north and tour some of the famous sites, but it wasn't possible. Our kids were having a hard time adjusting and some of the outings were difficult for them. Visiting the orphanages had been especially emotional, as we had to reassure them that we were not going to leave them there. Even a trip to the doctor's office triggered tantrums. When accompanied by Sedaya's frequent motion sickness and having to go to multiple pharmacies to find the proper medication, we were exhausted by the time we got back to our hotel.

We soon realized that the kids felt more secure when we stayed in our hotel room. We ventured out occasionally to take them swimming, which they loved, or to eat, but ate many of our meals in the room. With the high elevation of Addis Ababa and the nine-hour time change, we also had less energy than usual, so we were often asleep soon after the kids in the evenings.

Looking through the little photo albums we had brought for the kids was their favorite activity. They worked hard at learning each of our other kids' names and smiled when they pointed to the pictures of our house and its child-centered backyard. They loved hearing about the other kids, and although they seemed nervous about coming to Canada, they seemed excited to meet their new brothers and sisters.

For Mark and me, our reunion in Ethiopia hadn't gone as expected and there was still some tension between us, so we decided to go on a date. In some ways, it seemed absurd, but we knew that once we were back in Canada, it would be many months before we would leave Elijah and Sedaya with anyone else, so this would be our last opportunity for a long time to have some alone time.

We had read about an Italian restaurant that was supposed to be one of the best restaurants in the city, and made reservations. We got dressed in the best clothing we had brought, which was still fairly casual. We did our best to explain to the kids that they would be staying with Auntie Deanne while Mommy and Daddy went out to eat, but we would be coming back soon. We then ordered some food to the room for them.

It felt strange to be putting makeup on and preparing to go on a date while in Ethiopia, as we had come there to focus on the kids, not on our relationship, but I also knew that under the circumstances, it was best to nurture our marriage and spend some time together in preparation for all that was to come.

We took a taxi to Ristorante Castelli, an authentic Italian restaurant. In 1935, Italy had invaded Ethiopia and this restaurant had been founded by one of Mussolini's soldiers who decided to stay in Ethiopia and make his life there. We were seated in a small white room. I ordered a glass of wine and Mark got a beer. As we sipped our drinks and waited for our salads, I felt some of the tension evaporating. It felt wonderful to laugh and forget for a moment that our two newest children were having such a difficult time adjusting.

We kept the conversation light, not allowing ourselves to panic about what would happen once we were back home and had seven children to care for. It was such a nice treat to eat fresh salad, and our meals were divine! I ate a glorious pasta with truffle sauce while Mark enjoyed his homemade lasagna. I had always wanted to try truffle sauce but had never been able to afford it, but here the prices were such that I could indulge in this delicacy.

For dessert, we shared homemade Italian ice cream. We had feasted on one of the best Italian meals I had ever eaten and the bill made us smile even more. In total, our dinner of drinks, salads, main courses, and dessert totaled the equivalent of $36! Our date night put things back on track for us and gave us the energy boost we needed to get through the rest of the stay and the long trip back home. On the way back to the hotel, we each voiced our deepest fears and had very little comfort to offer each other, as we were both feeling the same way. With the kids' frequent tantrums and violent outbursts, we worried that maybe we had made a mistake, that we wouldn't be able to cope with all the kids once we returned home.

While we were at dinner, the kids had been treated like royalty by their Auntie Deanne. Together, they braided and beaded the hair on Sedaya's Cabbage Patch Doll, read books, did puzzles, played with play dough, and sang songs. Other than their supper, the kids did very well. When supper came to the room, they'd fought over the one egg. For both of them, their favorite meal was *doro wat* (chicken stew) and traditionally it is served with one hard-boiled egg. Every time they had it, an argument and meltdown over the egg would ensue. We tried to reason with them. We offered to cut the egg in half. We suggested taking turns eating the egg. No matter what, it always ended in hysterics. I later realized that we could have solved this problem very simply by requesting two eggs when we ordered the dish!

Being able to style Sedaya's hair was as fun as I had imagined it would be! The first morning I was there, I began to braid her hair, only having time to put a few braids in before we had to leave for the day. Every day, I added more braids until her whole head of hair had been braided and beaded. She loved every minute of it. She would often come to me and indicate that she wanted me to braid her hair by bringing me the bag of beads.

141

She loved the sound the beads made when she swished her head from side to side. I would add moisturizer and styling product before braiding and placing a few beads on the end.

The time we spent together every day, with Sedaya sitting close to me while I gently and lovingly combed the knots out of her hair, was very special. I was aware that my long-held dream of doing my daughter's hair had come true and I was thankful for being able to experience it. Sedaya would pick out which beads she wanted me to use and sit patiently, as I'm not a fast braider. It was a small bright spot every day that I looked forward to.

Sometimes when the kids were relaxed, we saw little pieces of their true personalities. Elijah was friendly and likable and was both easygoing and extremely competitive. He loved being able to watch soccer on the TV in our room and being read to. He most looked forward to swimming and to being able to see our drivers. It was obvious from observing his interaction with other Ethiopians that he was smart, confident, and outgoing.

twenty-one

OUR LAST DAY IN ETHIOPIA WAS VERY EMOTIONAL FOR ME. UNEXPECTEDLY, I felt conflicted about taking the kids away from the country of their birth. I had come to love Ethiopia and appreciate the complexities of the poverty and the challenges there. I knew that by coming to Canada, our children would be given opportunities that would not otherwise be possible for them, but they would also lose so much. They had already lost their birth family, the familiarity of their first home, and their original orphanage. Now they would lose the caregivers and friends at the Transition Home. Once we boarded the plane, they would be on the road to losing their language, their culture, and their home. I felt sad at leaving Ethiopia and couldn't imagine how they must be feeling. They were about to enter a world where everything was unfamiliar and no one would be able to speak their language or know their history.

I had brought books about airports and planes and every day we counted down the days until we would leave for Canada. I had explained as best I could that we would be taking one plane, then sleeping at a hotel, then a second plane, after which we would sleep at another hotel, and then the final plane which would take us home. I wasn't sure how much they understood. I knew they were afraid. The morning of our travel day, they were both very quiet. I ached to be able to comfort them and soothe their fears.

Elijah and Sedaya had both grown attached to our driver and to our guide. To the kids, they represented more than just men who were kind to them. They were also the link between us and them, as they had acted as our translators. Leaving them behind also meant leaving behind all effective communication with us.

As we got closer to the airport, Elijah especially grew more and more withdrawn. Elijah was so sad when saying goodbye to these wonderful men and acted as if they were betraying him by taking us to the place where he would be saying goodbye to everything he had ever known.

Juggling grouchy kids, the luggage, and our tickets and passports gave us a little preview of what was in store for us over the next few days. We were again grateful to have Deanne and her extra pair of hands. We managed to make it through security, although Sedaya refused to take her shoes off and had a huge tantrum just before we had to walk through. They wouldn't allow me to carry her through, but she refused to walk on her own. Instead, she lay on the ground, flailing about like a tuna on the shore. I was sweating and embarrassed by the bottleneck we were causing. I have no memory of how we were able to coax her through the metal detector, but somehow we all did end up on the other side.

The plane was delayed by a few hours and it seemed that with every minute of waiting, the kids' anxiety grew. Their bodies were tense and they were completely silent. We showed them other planes at the window of the terminal, played clapping songs with them, sang to them, and read to them, but their fears only increased. There was so much to be afraid of. They had never been on a plane before. However, I think that the mode of transportation was probably the smallest of their fears. I think the unknown of what awaited them in a strange new country was what drove them to stiffened silence.

Finally, we were finally able to board the plane and get the kids settled, but our troubles had only just begun. Mark sat with Elijah closer to the back of the plane and Sedaya sat next to me in the middle, with Deanne a row behind us. With their anxieties so heightened, the kids were wound tighter than a wind-up toy. It took almost nothing to set them off.

For Sedaya, having to put on the seatbelt sprung her loose. She fought me, kicking, biting, clawing, and screaming. Her scream was high-pitched and primal. I knew that her fears were being exposed. Deanne tried to help calm her down, but nothing either of us did or said brought her any comfort. It was as if putting on that seatbelt represented being complicit in going along with this plan to take her away from her world. She wanted none of it. The stewardess came by and explained again that the plane could not depart until my daughter's seatbelt was fastened. She mentioned that the full plane was already hours behind schedule. Flustered, I pleaded with Sedaya to let me attach it.

By then, I could hear a disturbance coming from further back in the plane as Elijah's wails made their way to my ears. Mark was engaged in his own struggle and could be of no assistance to me. I managed to get Deanne to distract flailing Sedaya for a millisecond while I did up the buckle on her seatbelt as loosely as it would go. I hid the evidence of the fastened seatbelt from her underneath a blanket after showing the stewardess that it was done up. Sedaya continued to kick, scream, and attempt to punch, hit, and bite me during takeoff and over the next hour or so until her screams subsided to sobs, which finally quieted to slumber. I wished for sleep myself, but I was kept awake by dread.

The current flight was the shortest of the three flights we had to make. I didn't know where I would pull the energy to complete the next day's thirteen-hour flight.

The plane was dark and mostly silent. Mark had managed to soothe Elijah by introducing him to the in-flight television, so the only noises I was aware of were the deep inhale and exhale of Sedaya's breaths and the pounding of my heart.

Arriving in Dubai this time was nothing like the time Deanne and I had entered the same airport a week earlier. I was hardly aware of the grandeur surrounding me, as my focus was on keeping the kids calm. Their eyes were huge and full of fear. Everything around them was new. As we went further into the airport, they even lost the comfort of seeing familiar features on the faces of other Ethiopians, as the others on our planes quickly went through customs and we waited for special visas for the kids.

With their passports stamped, we were able to make our way through the airport to the shuttle buses. By the time we arrived at the airport hotel, it was after 2:00 a.m. and the kids were weary and confused. Even though they were exhausted, their little bodies were wired with adrenaline and the fear kept them on edge. They jumped at movement and noise and their eyes darted furiously around the lobby as we waited for Mark to check us in. We made our way to the two rooms, Deanne's beside ours, and stood in the narrow hallway using the key cards to open the doors. We were quiet, knowing that lining the hallway were tiny rooms where travelers rested before boarding long flights to their ultimate destinations.

Once the door was open, Mark walked through and he beckoned the kids inside. Something about the room triggered panic in both Elijah and Sedaya. They began a frenzied escape attempt, doing anything necessary to get away from the doorway. They screamed the loudest and most pain-ridden cries I had ever heard. As we picked them up, they fought us as though their very lives depended on them not entering that small room.

In that hallway, in a foreign country in the early hours of the morning unsuccessfully trying to calm the kids down, we worried about the authorities being called by other hotel guests. How would we explain their distress? We thought that if we could only get the kids into the room, they would see that there was nothing to be afraid of. Between the three of us, we were able to muster up the strength to carry them through that doorway.

Once inside the room, though, their fears seemed to multiply. They behaved like wild, caged animals whose only hope for survival was escape. We held them as they bit us, kicked us, scratched us, punched us, hit us, and spit at us. There was no reasoning with them and they fed off each other. One would begin to calm down, but then become aware of the other's anguish and the screaming would begin anew. I tried to sing softly to them, but the notes were drowned out by their screams. Hours later, they fell asleep when fatigue finally won the battle. I was on the one bed holding Sedaya, with Mark on the other next to Elijah. We lay there in silence, each wondering if the decision to save these two children had ruined our family. What had we done?

In my mind, I questioned the sanity of our decision to add two more children to our already busy household. We had five more waiting for us back at home and Mark would be returning to work immediately, leaving me alone with all seven of them. Between Mark, Deanne, and me, we were barely able to cope with just these two. I also questioned the thought process behind adopting older children. These children had already experienced trauma, and it would take so much work to help them adjust, attach, and learn a new language. How had I ever thought I was capable of all this?

My fears threatened to engulf me. I could not cry. I dared not voice the deepest concerns of my inadequacies to Mark. Part of me wished that I was anywhere but in that room in Dubai. I wanted to give up. The next day's travel loomed, looking impossible after what we had just gone through. My body was still tired from the weeks leading up to Ethiopia, and my mind was a minefield of doubt. Before sleep finally descended upon me, I remembered Philippians 4:13—*"I can do all things through Christ who strengthens me"* (NKJV). It brought me peace.

In what felt like moments after I closed my eyes, the morning was upon us. The kids were still agitated and our carefully worded suggestions for them to get dressed brought more tantrums. We chose not to battle over anything that was not absolutely necessary, so their teeth didn't get brushed and their faces didn't get washed. Thankfully, I had braided and beaded all of Sedaya's hair when we were still in Ethiopia, so there was one less thing to worry about.

We ate quickly in the hotel restaurant and survived the glares of other patrons while the kids took turns having loud tantrums. Mark and I looked at each other a few times and didn't need to exchange words. We both feared what the day held.

The nightmare continued as the kids' fears were once again elevated at the airport. Mark, Deanne, and I had our own apprehensions and I'm sure the kids picked up on the tension. We got a bit of reprieve when Elijah discovered the moving walkways, which changed his mood considerably. Our plane was delayed, and during our wait we found someone who could speak Amharic. He overheard our butchered attempts at communication with the kids and approached us. We asked if he could try to allay our kids' fears and tell them what to expect on the plane ride. He spoke to them, and before long they were smiling and nodding. I was thankful to have this small blessing.

As we boarded the flight, I was keenly aware that there was no turning back. Once on that airplane, I would be stuck with two potentially screaming and raging children for more than thirteen hours. I took a deep breath and repeated to myself, "I can do all things through Christ who strengthens me."

During that flight, we experienced the most peaceful time we had known with the kids since we met them! They both settled in well. Elijah was enamored with the TV and remote. Sedaya slept much of the flight. I had packed their backpacks with snacks and toys and activities which we took out when boredom set in. I tried to explain what was to come next, to prepare them. I reminded them that after this, we would be going to a hotel, sleeping, then going on one more plane before we got home. The part that brought them the most comfort was when I talked

148

about the other kids being there at the airport after that last plane ride.

After a long but not unpleasant journey from Dubai to Toronto, we had a lengthy wait to get our bags before lining up to go through customs. We were a bit nervous for two reasons. We didn't know how long it would take to go through customs with two new citizens, and we weren't sure what documentation we would need to provide. We made sure we had everything ready.

Another reason for our nerves was that we expected there would be media waiting for us on the other side of customs. We had purposely booked our flight back to Edmonton the next day with an unaffiliated airline in an attempt to have a private homecoming with friends and family, but we knew that our flight information would be easy for the media to find. With all the interest in the story, we expected reporters to be on the other side of the gate. We were tired, disheveled, and had unpredictably behaved kids who were bewildered enough, so we hoped to slip into Canada unnoticed. The customs official was kind, and after looking over our paperwork and consulting with a superior, she stamped us through and Elijah and Sedaya were officially Canadians on Canadian soil! We exited the airport with no media in sight.

Our airport hotel was a few minutes away and I sensed that a good sleep was within my grasp. We prepared to load into a taxi van. While we were putting bags into the trunk, Elijah hopped into the front seat. In Ethiopia, he had enjoyed riding up front with our driver and had no reason to expect to do otherwise here. Mark tried to explain to him that he had to sit in the backseat. That did not go over well. Within minutes, Elijah was lying on the sidewalk, screaming and kicking anyone who came near him. He grabbed at whatever he could get his hands on and threw it at us. Mark and I gave each other a "Here we go again" look, followed quickly by a "What do we do?" glance.

Sedaya mistook his screaming as his being afraid of getting in the van. She then decided that if she stepped foot in that van, all kinds of evil would befall her, so she, too, refused to go in. The poor van driver stood to the side, looking like he wished he had never pulled up to us in the first place. A crowd began to gather, wondering what all the commotion was about. I worried that someone would think we were trying to kidnap these children when they saw white people trying to get screaming black children into a vehicle while they fought with all they had. I really expected the police to show up at any minute!

The whole scene might have been almost comical if not for the fresh memory of the night before. More than ten minutes later, with children who were now even more traumatized finally sitting in the backseat of the van, the driver mentioned that perhaps we should have Sedaya in a carseat. I laughed while I shook my head "no." I wasn't going to take on that battle today!

At this hotel, the kids easily went into the room with no evident fear. In the hotel restaurant, the kids tried French fries and ketchup for the first time and were not fans. My Auntie Judy and Uncle Ken, who live in Toronto, arrived while we were eating and then we all went back up to our room for a visit. They were amazed at how many English words the kids had already learned. The kids were a bit curious about the newcomers, but stuck pretty close to Mark, Deanne, and I. Before they left, my aunt and uncle went down to the front desk and generously paid for our room!

We all slept well that night. Staying overnight there allowed the kids to begin adjusting to the time change.

In the morning, Deanne had to leave early for the airport, as she was flying to Vancouver. We had explained to the kids that Auntie Deanne would not be coming on the last flight with us but would be coming to visit them at our house in a few months. It was clear that morning that they had not really understood us and were confused by what was happening. When Deanne tried to say goodbye to them, they wouldn't look her in the eye or go to her. They had grown so close to her, and now they felt betrayed. After so many losses, they were experiencing another. I grieved for them. Deanne was so sad to leave them like that.

After Deanne left, Elijah had a meltdown about getting dressed. Sedaya and I went down to the restaurant to start eating breakfast, and once Elijah calmed down, he and Mark joined us. I knew most of the Amharic words for standard breakfast food and the kids seemed relieved that familiar food was available in Canada. I talked to them about what kinds of foods we would have at our house. I had made a call from Ethiopia to my sister-in-law Stephanie and asked her to stock our kitchen with a few of the kids' favorite foods like mangos, bananas, and Corn Flakes. This way, they could have some comfort food right away.

The mood after Deanne left was somber, but once we got through security at the airport and were waiting to board our last flight, there was a shift. The air lightened and I could sense a hesitant excitement in the kids, especially Elijah. He asked repeatedly if Mackenzie, Jonah, Gracelyn, Josiah, and Eliana would be at the airport when we got to Canada. We hadn't wanted to confuse the kids by telling them that Toronto was in Canada, too, so we had referred to the Edmonton stop as "Canada." We assured him that all his new brothers and sisters would be there to greet him and that they were so happy that he was coming. Elijah took out their pictures while we waited and practiced saying their names. He did this again on the plane. Sedaya slept most of the leg from Toronto to Edmonton and seemed relaxed.

The crew aboard the West Jet flight was wonderful. Once they learned that we had just adopted Elijah and Sedaya from Ethiopia, the news was passed along. They brought the kids coloring sheets and blankets and asked us questions and offered their congratulations. One flight attendant crouched down beside me and shared with me her story of being adopted from another country as a youngster and her journey back to visit that country as an adult. She expressed to me how grateful she was to the couple who had adopted her and to the woman who had chosen to give her life. She wished us luck.

We were the last to disembark the plane, as the flight attendants had made arrangements for our kids to be able to go and see the cockpit and meet the captains. This was such a thrill for Elijah!

twenty-two

CHAPTER

ON THE AFTERNOON OF AUGUST 6, 2009, MARK AND I ARRIVED AT THE Edmonton International Airport with Elijah and Sedaya on our third day of travel. We were exhausted and relieved to be home.

We could hardly wait to see our other kids and finally take Elijah and Sedaya home. We walked through the automatic doors to a wall of reporters and camera flashes. It took us aback. Beyond the media, though, were over thirty of our friends and family who had come to welcome us home and to welcome Elijah and Sedaya to Canada.

When they saw us, a cheer rose up among the crowd. Tears formed in my eyes as Mackenzie, Jonah, Gracelyn, Josiah, and Eliana ran forward to embrace us and to greet their new siblings.

We had made it. We were home.

twenty-three

LATE THAT AFTERNOON, AFTER THE EXCITEMENT HAD DIED DOWN AND THE last of our extended family had gone home, I stepped onto the deck and was met with the sight of all seven of my children playing in the backyard. I remembered the morning that I had looked into the yard and cried, wondering if Elijah and Sedaya would ever have the chance to run and laugh and play here, the chance to just be kids.

I could hardly believe the events that had transpired leading up to this day. I thought of all those who had prayed for Elijah and Sedaya's safety and homecoming. I thought of those who had cared for our five other kids while we were away. I thought of our friends who had organized fundraisers. I thought of our Leon Benoit, our MP, and Lottie at his office whose incredible work had pushed to expedite the visas to bring our kids home, and of the staff at the High Commission in Nairobi who had worked tirelessly. I thought of the staff at Alberta Children's Services. I thought of the caregivers at the Transition Home, who had looked after our kids without pay. I thought of the other adoptive parents who had rallied around us. I thought of the company who had donated funds to protect the children affected in Ethiopia. I thought of a community who had rallied around our family. I thought of those who had set up our house while we were gone. I thought of strangers who had showed us kindness and compassion. And when I thought of a God who had allowed us the privilege of becoming parents again, I was overcome with emotion.

I watched my children play, watched as Elijah and Sedaya's hesitation melted away. They kicked balls, ran on the lawn, romped on the swing set, jumped on the trampoline, and laughed easily. I could see it in their faces… they knew that they were home.

epilogue

IT HAS BEEN MORE THAN A YEAR AND A HALF SINCE THAT DAY WHEN WE finally landed in Edmonton and united our family. Elijah and Sedaya are thriving. They are speaking English almost as though they have spoken it all their lives. They have learnt to trust us and have attached to us.

In the first few months home, there were many struggles due to insecure attachment, their fears, and limitations in our communication. There were tantrums and tears. There was jetlag and exhaustion. There were parasites and fungi. There were adjustments that had to be made by the other kids. It would be a lie to say that we got to where we are at now without a lot of hard work. It wasn't easy. Elijah went through eleven months of play therapy and many months of attachment therapy. Sedaya's attachment therapy came later.

In the beginning, there were moments when we were overwhelmed, and even moments when we almost wished for our old lives back, but then we began to see glimmers of what our new life could be. As the kids came to trust us, their attachment to us grew. We discovered that Elijah is a very affectionate boy with a soft heart who especially loves animals and babies. We discovered that Sedaya loves to help me and spend time with me. In many ways, her personality is the most like mine out of all our kids!

156

We slowly slipped into a new routine and very quickly felt like the family we were on paper. It has been a true privilege to get to know these two uniquely wonderful children, to see inside them and watch their personalities emerge. They are awesome little people who fill our home with laughter and only add to our family.

There was a point on this adoption journey when our motivation had been primarily to give a home to children who needed homes, but we have now discovered that it was actually us who needed them. We didn't know it then, but our family wasn't complete without our son Elijah and our daughter Sedaya.

Before the addition of our Ethiopian children, our family was less unified. Our older boys were considerably older than our other three children and the two groups didn't interact much. Gracelyn and Josiah, our artificial twins,[2] were inseparable, which often left out our youngest, Eliana. Through this adoption experience, Mackenzie and Jonah, our older boys, have become more involved with all their younger siblings and the younger five, comprised now of artificial triplets Gracelyn, Josiah, and Elijah, and artificial twins Eliana and Sedaya, can usually be found playing all together. This experience has shaped us and strengthened us and brought us all closer together. A number of months after we brought the kids home, Mark said to me, "That was the best thing we've ever done for our family!" I couldn't agree more!

Elijah and Sedaya have made our lives richer, not harder. They have taught me more than I have taught them. They have given me more than I have given them. They are amazing, resilient, priceless children and I'm proud to call myself their mom. I'm so thankful that they are no longer orphans. They are ours. Our lives have truly been changed forever by this experience.

---

[2]Artificial twins is a term used among adoptive families to identify non-biological siblings who are less than eleven months apart.

A lot has happened in our family and in the adoption world since bringing Elijah and Sedaya home.

Since our adoption, rules surrounding adoptions from Ethiopia have changed considerably. One of the biggest changes is that adoptive parents are now required to make two trips to Ethiopia, one to stand before a judge in court and answer questions about their intentions and suitability to meet the needs of their child or children, and a second to pick up their child or children once a visa is issued. Ethiopia continues to look for ways to make intercountry adoptions as ethical as possible.

That determined group of prospective adoptive parents who formed FIA (Families of Imagine Adoption) after the agency's bankruptcy were able to come up with a plan to resurrect the agency. On July 30, 2009, Imagine Adoption creditors voted to restructure the agency, and on September 21, 2009, the majority of creditors voted to accept a proposal which would allow many waiting parents to be able to continue with their adoptions.

In December of 2009, the first referral of the newly restructured agency came in! Since that time, many Ethiopian children have been adopted by parents who originally thought their dreams of adopting were lost the day of the bankruptcy. This is nothing short of a miracle! To date, more than a hundred children have been referred since the bankruptcy. In 2011, Mission of Tears took over the remaining Imagine Adoption client files to bring them to completion.

My friend Ruth, who was right behind us in line for a sibling referral when the bankruptcy happened, has had a long road, but her family accepted a referral in November 2010 of an adorable five-year-old boy and his sweet three-year-old sister. The first day I ever heard Ruth's voice was when she phoned to tell me the news of their referral, and I cried at the checkout in Ikea! Ruth and her husband finally brought their new son and daughter home to Canada in June 2011, more than three years after their dossier first arrived in Ethiopia.

My friend Karen, who adopted two girls who grew up in the same village as Elijah and Sedaya, brought her family to our house for a visit and it was interesting to watch the four kids who had last seen each other at the Transition Home react to seeing each other again in Canada! It is special for our kids to have contact with some of the kids they knew in Ethiopia.

Arnica Rowan, the woman who was with us the day we spent at Faya Orphanage, is now the president of the Vulnerable Children Society, a non-profit organization that raises money and awareness in Canada for vulnerable children in African nations. The Vulnerable Children Society is now the sponsorship facilitator for Faya Orphanage. Arnica also facilitates Okanagan Families with Children from Africa. She and her husband are settled at home with their girls and are now pursuing another African adoption.

Shelley and her husband have adjusted to life with both of their boys. Sometimes when I see their Ethiopian son, I am brought back to the days when Shelley and I were helping each other in the fight to get our children home. I can't help but smile to see their son in a family who loves him so obviously and advocates for him so strongly. Shelley and her husband are just the parents he needed.

Last year, we took the kids to Mannville, Alberta to visit Leon Benoit, our MP, and his assistant Lottie. We wanted to be able to thank them in person for everything they had done to help our kids come to Canada as quickly as possible, and for our kids to be able to shake hands with people working in our government who care about their constituents and their families.

In April 2011, after an almost two-year investigation by the RCMP, founder and former Executive Director of Imagine Adoptions Sue Hayhow and Imagine's former General Manager and Chief Financial Officer Rick Hayhow were arrested for fraud. The pair was charged with breach of trust, six counts of fraud over $5,000, three counts of fraud under $5,000, and an additional count each of fraud under $5,000.

On the day I heard of the arrests, all kinds of emotions resurfaced for me. Although the agency had been resurrected and many children in Ethiopia had as a result found their way to loving families, for some waiting families, the stress and financial burden of Imagine's bankruptcy were too much and their adoption dreams ended on that very sad day in July 2009. There were also children in the Transition Home at that time whose paperwork was not complete and who had to be sent back to uncertain fates at their originating orphanages.

We also now know that for a period of about six weeks, our children and the other children at the Transition Home were fed only one small meal of a simple grain each day. There had been no money for gas to drive to appointments, so when Elijah got a gash on his forehead that should have required stitches, he didn't get medical attention. The caregivers and other staff had fed our children with their own money, though they had little to spare as they had not been paid in months. So much destruction had occurred at the hands of a woman who professed faith, who claimed a love and compassion for orphans, and who stood on a platform of "our unique, total love approach."

Over the months after we first got home with our kids, I struggled with anger and feelings of helplessness and guilt. I felt like somehow I should have known that something wasn't right. I felt stupid for trusting someone else with the care of my children without doing more research or asking more questions. I felt angry about the amount of money we'd been forced to spend to ensure that they were well cared for, only to find out that they hadn't been.

With each new piece of information, I struggled to forgive this woman who had hurt my children. I struggled about what I would tell them someday about evil in this world and how that evil had been the reason they'd worried for themselves and for each other during their short months at the Transition Home.

I had hoped for an arrest, thinking it would bring some closure and a feeling that justice was coming, but when I heard of the arrest I felt only sadness. Nothing done to this woman by our justice system would take the pain away from my children. No jail time would give the families who could not continue with their adoptions their long-awaited child. No financial restitution she could potentially pay would cover the true expense of what her actions had cost.

The arrest has forced me to begin the hard work of forgiveness anew.

As for that Disneyworld trip we'd planned to take as our last vacation as a family of seven? In September of 2009, just one month after returning home with the kids, nine of us boarded a plane en route for Florida! Obviously, we considered canceling the trip, but as we were using nonrefundable points, we knew it could be years before we could consider going again. We didn't want the other kids to resent their new siblings for being the reason they didn't get to go on the trip they'd been looking forward to, so we set off together.

It was a challenge for me, as Mark had to work from the room everyday and Elijah and Sedaya still didn't speak much English, but the looks on their faces when they saw the Magic Kingdom made it almost worth it! For kids who were still fascinated by ceiling fans, meeting Mickey Mouse, going on rides, and putting their feet in the ocean were beyond their wildest imaginations! It turned out that Mark's decision to bring our kids home as Canadian citizens was fortunate again, as it meant that we were able to get them Canadian passports in time for the trip.

In November of 2010, Mark returned to Ethiopia with our oldest son Mackenzie, who was fifteen at the time. They brought donations to Faya Orphanage and played with the kids there. Mackenzie was able to meet a young girl who had made a big impression on both Mark and me our first time at Faya. The two of them also visited the first orphanage that Elijah and Sedaya had lived in. The kids there surrounded Mackenzie and were so excited to play with him.

While in Ethiopia, Mark and Mackenzie made the long trip to the village that Elijah and Sedaya were from and took pictures that will be a lifelong treasure for our kids. The mud-walled, grass-roofed, one-room shelter that Elijah and Sedaya once called home stood in stark contrast to their new house in Canada. They also went to Lalibela and Axum, places Mark had hoped to travel to on our previous trip. They experienced more of the rich culture and warm hospitality that typify Ethiopia and confirmed that the country and its people are forever ingrained in the fabric of our family.

Adoption is one of the most complex things in life. The truth about adoption is that, though it is beautiful and a miracle, it is, at its root, about loss. By nature, it is imperfect. Without loss, adoption couldn't exist. For me, when I think about adoption, the words that usually come to mind are "miracle," "gift," "blessing," "God," "beautiful," "forever," "love," "claiming," "family," and "beginning." All of those can be true, but before they are spoken, other words like "orphan," "abandon," "loss," "heartache," "choice," "broken," "separate," "give up," "taken," "empty," "infertility," "grieve," "addiction," "waiting," or "end" need to be heard. And yet, the families who are brought together through adoption are not done so by accident. Yes, in God's perfect plan, mothers can care for the children born to them and there is no infertility, no need for adoption to exist. Unfortunately, we live in an imperfect world and the need for adoption does exist. God is able to work that into His plan.

One morning, I was blindsided by some unbelievably hard questions from a distraught Sedaya, who at six years old wanted to talk to me about people who don't have clean water or enough food and who die and don't know Jesus. We talked about it a bit, and then she looked at me and said, "When you little girl, your mommy have food?"

Tears sprung to my eyes immediately and I felt the weight of this precious girl's early years and the impact that hunger will always have for her. I explained to her that when I was a little girl, my mommy had enough food for us to eat, to which she replied, "And her can eat too?" More tears.

As a mother, I cannot imagine having to choose which of my kids to feed because there isn't enough to go around, or feeding my kids tiny amounts and trying to hide from them that I'm not eating to try to save them. I cannot imagine as a mother knowing my kids are going to bed with empty tummies and knowing that there's nothing I can do about it. My heart aches for all the mothers around the world who are faced with this reality today.

Later, Sedaya and I talked a bit about how her first mommy loved Jesus, how I love Jesus and how Sedaya loves Jesus, and how someday she will be with both her mommies in Heaven. She was happy to hear that, but it still weighed heavily on her that other people who have no food don't know Jesus. She asked me if we could add that into our homeschool prayer every morning.

She also asked me why we have so much food in Canada when there isn't enough food in Africa. She cried. I'm glad that my kids have compassion for others. I wish these hard questions had easy answers, though. I wish it were as simple as just sending some of our excess from Canada to Africa. I wish it were as simple as the prayer of a child. And maybe it is. Or at least, maybe it will be someday.

Our family has been changed by our international adoption. We have gotten involved in fundraising for Hope International, Faya Orphanage, and adoptions for other families. We are teaching our kids to have an outlook on the world as more of a global community, and hopefully we'll instill in them a desire to see what's going on in their community and the world and become involved. We are already seeing the fruits of this, as they happily give their toys to be sold at garage sales to raise funds for a friend's adoption and ran a concession to raise money for Faya. I am proud of the compassion and kindness that I can see developing in our children.

We are now appreciative not only of the gift of being born in such an affluent country, but also of the responsibility that comes with it. International adoption doesn't just give homes to orphaned, abandoned, or impoverished children; it opens the eyes and hearts of the families who come to see firsthand the worldwide orphan crisis. We know of adoptive families who have gone on to partner with orphanages in the third-world, start non-profit corporations to raise money, partner with established organizations to bring clean water projects to the villages their children were born in, raise awareness of those around them, host an annual fundraising triathlon, and volunteer their time and services in developing countries. The ripple effect of international adoption is simply too large to be measured.

After hearing from others of their frustration in finding adoption resources for Canadians, and experiencing the same myself, I started an online adoption resource called Adoption Magazine. One of my other reasons was in response to the tremendous support I have received in the adoption community and the information that I was able to access thanks to blogs where families had shared honestly about adoption. Many paint an unrealistic picture of adoption, which contributes to new adoptive parents feeling isolated. I wanted to create a venue where truths about adoption, attachment, post-adoption depression, therapeutic parenting, loss in adoption, and stories of struggle would be shared. I also wanted to help parents by allowing them to pass along ideas, and for people to know that they're not alone. Of course, another huge reason was to advocate for adoption and orphan care. I can still feel my heart being pulled towards adoption, but at this time in my life, I feel it pulled towards adoption advocacy and post-adoption support of others.

We often get asked if our family is now complete. I cannot answer that. When we first arrived home with Elijah and Sedaya and it was hard, I felt like I was in over my head. At that time, I would have answered with certainty that our family was complete with seven kids. Now, more than a year and a half later, life is manageable and most days are a lot of fun. There are days, though, when I still feel overwhelmed or busy. Our daughter Gracelyn still struggles with her lung condition and there are days, and even weeks and months, when her care takes over our lives. At those times, I feel like seven is enough. But the truth is, I don't know the answer, because I feel at peace leaving it in God's hands. I marvel at how He chose Elijah and Sedaya for our family, and us for them. We are what they needed in so many ways, and they are the perfect fit for us. I can hardly remember our family without them, and when I look back, I can see clearly that they are what was missing.

If you look only at logic, then we will probably not adopt again. Logic dictates that seven children is, nowadays, in North America, a huge family. Logic dictates that seven children is a huge expense. Logic dictates that I have a husband who is much more rational than I am and is less apt to make decisions based purely on emotion. Logic dictates a lot, but it doesn't dictate the size of our family. For now, we are done. That could mean that we are done forever. Or it could mean that tomorrow we will start the process towards another adoption. Because God trumps all logic in my mind and in my heart. Our family size will be determined by God. He has called us to adopt and I know that He is still working in our family.

That doesn't necessarily mean that He will add children to it though. If God did lead us to add more children through adoption, they would be as much of a blessing as each of our other seven are. Our lives would not be as rich or as fun or as crazy or as full of love were it not for each of our seven children, each and every one.

Adopting older children is different in many ways than our previous experiences with adoption. Though I have found it a bit sad that I missed out on many firsts in their lives, such as their first steps and smiles, it has been a joy to be there to see the look on their faces the first time they ate ice cream or the first time they saw twinkling Christmas lights. With our previous adoptions, we received our kids as newborns or babies, so I didn't expect that I would be able to attach as much to older children. I knew that over time they would feel like my kids, but I thought it would take a long time. Secretly, I worried that maybe I would never be able to love them with the fierceness and passion with which I love my other kids.

I wish I had known then what I know now… that sometimes just thinking about or talking about Elijah or Sedaya can bring me to tears, that the first time I went away without them, I missed them with a hollowness that is difficult to describe, that they are a part of me. I wish I had known that even with kids who were seven and four the first time I held their hands in mine, I would be forever changed by their love.